A PRACTICAL GUIDE FOR
PARENTS, TEACHERS AND COACHES

UNDERSTANDING CHILDREN AND TEENS

Judy Bartkowiak

First published by Free Association Books.

Copyright © 2020 Judy Bartkowiak

The author's rights are fully asserted. The rights of
Judy Bartkowiak to be identified as the author of
this work has been asserted by her in accordance with the
Copyright, Designs and Patents Act 1988
A CIP Catalogue of this book is available from
the British Library

ISBN: 978-1-911-38350-5

Typeset by
Typo•glyphix
www.typoglyphix.co.uk

Cover illustration and concept by LittlePinkPebble
Technical design by Candescent

Printed and bound in England

For parents, teachers and coaches,
all over the world.

– Believe in yourself and trust your intuition.

This is a really important time in history when you have the opportunity to make a huge difference in children's lives. Do it!

CONTENTS

Contents

FOREWORD

Judy Bartkowiak is an international NLP and EFT Trainer, Therapist and Author specialising in working with children, teens, parents and families. Her passion is to show her clients how to move from a stuck state of low self-esteem, depression, fear and anxiety, anger or grief into a state of flow where what they want and need is possible.

She is trained and experienced in Neuro Linguistic Programming (NLP), Emotional Freedom Technique (EFT), Picture Tapping Technique (PTT), Matrix Reimprinting and Mindfulness. Before becoming a therapist, she worked in children's market research for companies such as LEGO, Mattel, Aardman, Hasbro and the BBC.

In writing this book, Judy wants to share her expertise and to empower those who love children by giving them a cornucopia of techniques that will enable them to express themsclves and to build emotional intelligence and resilience. It is her belief that when they believe in themselves with unconditional love and acceptance, they will achieve all they wish for in life.

Judy is the author of a number of NLP books which may be helpful should you wish to delve further into NLP or apply NLP to yourself.

o *NLP Workbook* – comprehensive introduction to NLP concepts, theory, and techniques with questions to get you implementing the learning for yourself.
o *Self-Esteem Workbook* – applies NLP principles to all aspects of self-esteem guiding you through the exercises to increase your self-esteem.
o *Secrets of the NLP Masters* – 50 chapters covering applied NLP techniques and principles to all areas of your life; sport, family, health, friendships, work and relationships.

o *Be a happier parent with NLP* – definitive parenting guide taking you through every NLP principle and technique so you can apply it as a parent then the second part covers specific situations such as moving house, moving school, new baby, etc.

o Engaging NLP series of workbooks for children, tweens, teens, parents, teachers, work, back to work, pregnancy & childbirth, weight loss.

You can get in touch with her via her website **www.nlpfamily.com**

INTRODUCTION

When I started to write this book, pre Covid-19 in January 2020, it was my intention to share with you all my experience and learnings so that you would have a wide range of tools and modalities at your fingertips as professionals working with children, teens, parents and families. It had not been my intention to write for parents as I had done with *Be a happier parent with NLP*.

Then Covid-19 turned our lives upside down. We all had to face almost wartime restrictions on our liberty, our finances and our ability to work. Schools closed and children were home-schooled while parents tried to continue working with nobody able to draw on extended families and friends for support. Many of us lost our jobs, homes and livelihood. Thousands lost loved ones. It would be fair to say that we all struggled, along with other families, all over the world.

As I was writing the book, parents were telling me how they and their families were suffering, how they were experiencing mental and emotional problems they hadn't had before and they didn't know what to do. I realised that what I was writing for professionals was also relevant for parents, many of whom would, in any case, be working in a professional capacity with children. I also recognised that teachers were also facing extreme challenges and would continue to do so for many months or even years. So, parents and teachers, this book is very much written with you in mind.

Whether you use these exercises for your own children or for those you work with, they are all fun to do and yield great insight. They enable healing through showing children and teens that they have other possibilities. They are no longer stuck and can change their patterns.

My guiding principles when working with children are:

- o Observe the body language
- o Listen and notice the language patterns
- o Listen specifically for the limiting beliefs
- o Be curious about where they might have the skills to overcome them
- o Find their models of excellence
- o Help them 'join up the dots'
- o Make the learning and skills 'portable' so they don't need me

Joining up the dots may be through:

- o Reflecting back using 'clean language'
- o Feedback of a pattern you've noticed
- o Guiding them in an exercise which enables them to disassociate and see the pattern for themselves
- o Addressing a limiting belief through a technique from NLP or EFT

The analogy I use is this:

Imagine your client is stuck in the mud. They can't get out on their own, and by holding out your hand to them, they can make their first few steps until they are back on the dry ground where they can run and play again.

You will have your own metaphor or analogy of how you work with your child clients or with your own child, and I think it's helpful to have one, because there can be a tendency when you love children to 'rescue' them rather than coach them. As parents, we do still need to have access to that inner coach as children move towards independence. This is a time when you can't be 'fixing' or 'rescuing them' and they need to be forming their own coping strategies.

Finally, it is my intention that this book contains all the skills and expertise I have acquired over the last 20 years or so while working with children. We continue to learn all the time, and I share what I know with my students. You can book training courses with me via my website **www.nlpfamily.com** and I have listed resources at the back for modalities that I mention but in which I am not an expert.

DEMYSTIFYING THE ACRONYMS
NLP, EFT, PTT, CLEAN LANGUAGE AND MATRIX REIMPRINTING

Let's get the theory out of the way quickly! Whilst I am enormously grateful to Richard Bandler and John Grinder for developing a life philosophy that is as relevant today as it was in the 1960s when they came up with the name 'Neuro Linguistic Programming', I wish to goodness they had named it something more accessible to parents and those who work with children!

1. NLP STANDS FOR NEURO LINGUISTIC PROGRAMMING.

'Neuro' is all our thoughts, experiences, beliefs, expectations, inner chatter that we use to filter what we experience through our senses. So, just as we have all had different parents and experienced different early years, everyone's filters will be different. This means that each of us can experience the same event but make it mean something different.

'Linguistic' is how we respond verbally and non-verbally. Our facial expressions, body language and of course the words we use, are based on what we have made the event mean to us: our internal representation of it. The linguistic part is how we then present this version of it to the outside world.

'Programming' is what happens next. We tend to repeat patterns because they are based on our map of the world. So, even when we don't get the result we want, we still keep repeating the patterns because our neural pathways have learnt this and it's familiar.

When we understand the structure of this programme – the beliefs and thoughts behind it and the language pattern – we are then able to change it. The focus of NLP is to know what we want and to understand how we can achieve it.

Bandler and Grinder consulted with many others to create their principles: Virginia Satir, Milton Erickson, Fritz Perls, Gregory Bateson, Alfred Korzybski and Noam Chomsky.

I'd like to share with you some of Virginia Satir's work as a Family Therapist, specifically her Therapeutic Beliefs taken from 'The Satir Model'. You may recognise these later in the NLP Presuppositions.

1. Change is possible. Even if external change is limited, internal change is possible.
2. Parents do the best they can at any given time.
3. We all have the internal resources we need to cope successfully and to grow.
4. We have choices, especially in terms of responding to stress instead of reacting to situations.
5. Therapy needs to focus on health and possibilities instead of pathology.
6. Hope is a significant component or ingredient for change.
7. People connect on the basis of being similar and grow on the basis of being different.
8. A major goal of therapy is to become our own choice makers.
9. We are all manifestations of the same life force.
10. Most people choose familiarity over comfort, especially during times of stress.
11. The problem is not the problem; coping is the problem.
12. Feelings belong to us. We all have them.
13. People are basically good. To connect with and validate their own self-worth, they need to find their own inner treasure.
14. Parents often repeat the familiar patterns from their growing up times, even if the patterns are dysfunctional.
15. We cannot change past events, only the effects they have on us.
16. Appreciating and accepting the past increases our ability to manage our present.

17. One goal in moving toward wholeness is to accept our parental figures as people and meet them at their level of personhood rather than only in their roles.
18. Coping is the manifestation of our level of self-worth. The higher our self-worth, the more wholesome our coping.
19. Congruence and high self-esteem are major goals in the Satir model.
20. Healthy human relationships are built on equality of value.

I think you'll agree with me, whether as a parent, or a practitioner, teacher, or other professional working with children, that these beliefs from Satir are still very much relevant to us today, even in a world that is so very different from the world she knew when she wrote them.

2. EFT STANDS FOR EMOTIONAL FREEDOM TECHNIQUE OR 'TAPPING' AS IT IS MORE WIDELY KNOWN

EFT is an Energy Healing Modality. It is based on ancient Eastern Medicine and focuses on our awareness of the emotions as we experience them inside our body. We first feel emotions in our body – butterflies in our tummy, a sick feeling, tightness in the chest, sweaty palms and so on. Our brain tries to make sense of them and, as parents or teachers, we might ask, 'Why do you feel like that?' Children have already asked themselves this question and have no idea.

What has happened is that something has triggered their 'fight/flight/freeze' response. The amygdala basically acts like a smoke alarm when all that has happened is that, metaphorically, we have simply 'burnt the toast'. This is a reaction to something much deeper in the subconscious, and could well be the manifestation of a core limiting belief they have formed about themselves, such as 'I'm stupid' or 'No-one cares what I think' or 'Mummy doesn't love me'. These beliefs are formed in utero and in early childhood when we don't even have that reasoning ability. This is why we don't know why we feel it, because it doesn't make any sense logically. It was a perception we picked up from our environment at a time when we couldn't understand anything other than our own need for survival.

Let me share with you a very simple exercise that you can do for yourself right now and use for your children and clients. I find it a great way to introduce ourselves, and those we love, to the idea that our emotions live in our body and have colour.

Exercise
Draw an outline of a human body.

Now write down alongside it the first emotions or feeling words that come to mind. Children tend to write: sad, happy, frustrated or angry. Yours may be different.

Alongside each one, make a mark with a felt pen to show the colour that comes to mind when you think of that emotion. Now you have a code.

Now, for each emotion, colour in the part of the body where you feel that emotion. Take your time, there may be several places.

Tapping uses the acupressure or tapping points along meridian lines in the body which connect the organs. We combine tapping on the points with saying the negative feeling we want to get rid of i.e. sad, cross, fed up, tired, lonely. EFT practitioners feel we are connecting with what's blocking us and allowing it to go. We are clearing the blockage.

The process is quite simple which is why children love it so much – they can easily do it themselves.

Even very young children can do simple tapping on themselves or on their teddy bear. As they tap on their bear, for whatever they are feeling they are getting the benefit. They might say "my bear is afraid of the dark" or "he feels all alone" as they tap him on his face and hands. This is called 'surrogate tapping'. When you, the parent or practitioner, tap along as well they are getting additional 'borrowed benefits' – as are we, of course. In fact, tapping as a group, tapping as a class in school, as a family, can be very powerful.

Once children know how to tap, they can use it whenever they need to feel relaxed.

3. PTT – STANDS FOR PICTURE TAPPING TECHNIQUE

This technique combines EFT Tapping with Clean Language and Art Therapy. The child connects to their negative feeling and then draws their feelings on the paper, giving each drawing a title. We focus on the title then on the individual elements drawn on the paper e.g. 'red circle', black wiggly line', and so on. Typically, it will take about 5 -7 drawings to clear an issue.

It is a great technique when you want to work 'content-free' which might be helpful with teenagers in particular, or if your child prefers not to tell you what they are worried about. This way you can help them without them having to reveal the details.

I find that sometimes once the issue has cleared, the clients then feel quite relaxed about telling you what they were tapping on, but they don't have to.

4. MATRIX REIMPRINTING

I do not intend to cover this in much detail, as it is best used by those who have been trained in it by Karl Dawson who created this modality. The principle is that we use EFT Tapping to uncover the emotions, and the belief behind them, to go back in time to when they were first imprinted in our first six years. Beliefs can also be imprinted in utero, passed down from ancestors or even from a past life.

Some children can remember very clearly when they first believed that they were 'not important' or 'believed mummy loved their younger sibling more than them'. For others, the memory comes as we tap on how they feel now. In fact, when they guess, it will often turn out to be correct (when we talk to their mum) because those guesses come from our subconscious.

In this book I am showing you how to use The Time Line (which is a standard NLP technique) to encourage children and teenagers to walk back in time as they revisit their inner child and the key events of their life.

5. CLEAN LANGUAGE

This is a communication process initially created by David Grove, a counselling psychologist in the 1980s, and further developed by James Lawley and Penny Tompkins in the 1990s. It is a way of questioning which uses the other person's own words and blends them with a set of questions which have been designed to be as free as possible from assumption, thus respecting their 'map of the world' rather than imposing one's own.

The cleanest language is just a querying look or repeating the last word your child said. Other clean languages phrases are: "tell me more", "in what way?". We are using the word 'clean' to mean that we just echo the child's words rather than adding our own.

(1)

HOW TO BE PRACTICALLY PERFECT IN EVERY WAY
THE NLP BELIEFS OF EXCELLENCE OR PRESUPPOSITIONS.

When Richard Bandler and John Grinder developed NLP, at its centre was 'Modelling.' It's a skill we are born with; it's our survival skill and part of our reptilian brain which ensures that we are fed and not abandoned by our primary carer. As a baby, children watch their parents and older siblings, picking up how to stand, walk, say words, they learn how to be a little human. They repeat actions until they get them right and they persist because they can observe the model of how it is possible. When they go to school there are many more models of excellence from which they can copy and learn. We are told not to compare ourselves with others but children do this naturally and this is all part of the learning process. What we should really be showing children is how to watch others and learn to do it themselves rather than watch and tell themselves that this person is somehow better than them. They are not; they have simply mastered something we need to learn.

The beliefs of excellence, or 'presuppositions', is a set of beliefs that support modelling. Whilst we can copy what others do and get the physical steps by observing and questioning, what we still need is the underlying belief. There is an entire chapter on the Modelling process so you can practise it yourselves, teach it to the children you care for and use it with your clients to show them how to model their own excellence, as well as the excellence of those they admire. In this chapter, we are learning how to share a more general set of beliefs that can be applied in every part of our life. They are extremely important for us in working with children and being their models of excellence as parents, teachers and coaches.

Bandler and Grinder studied models of excellence across a wide range of disciplines and were curious. 'What if we could come up with a list of beliefs that would code excellence such that whatever we are doing, by applying this set of beliefs, we would achieve the best results?'

And that is what they did.

I use these in a number of ways

1. AS A GENTLE REMINDER COMMENT

A child may comment on something that another child or parent does that they find really annoying or impressive, and I may ask, 'And how could that also be true for you as well?' going on to talk about the 'if you spot it you've got it' belief.

They might demonstrate, in a story they are recounting, how something happens, and they always respond in a certain way that you can see isn't working for them. I might ask, 'And does this work?' When they admit that it doesn't, I might say, 'The person with the most flexibility controls the system,' going on to explain that when we have many options of response we have more power and control over the outcome.

Do you see, then, how we can pop one of these wonderful beliefs into a conversation with a child or teen?

2. AS A SPECIFIC LESSON

Each one of these beliefs of excellence can be a session in itself. I've done many sessions just on one, such as, 'There's no failure, only feedback,' or 'You have all the resources you need,' but they are all so rich and life changing.

Teachers, you can spread the beliefs of excellence across a term programme using the first session to introduce NLP, take one belief per lesson and use the final lesson as a feedback session on which they found most useful as a belief to take on in their day to day life. Maybe think about setting up a debate with one side arguing that one is the most useful and the opposing team fighting for the other most popular belief.

Each belief could lend itself to a drama lesson, acting out how it could be applied in everyday school life scenarios.

They could form the basis for an art project.

I'm sure you have lots of ideas!

Mind and body are one

If you try you won't succeed

The person with the most flexibility controls the system

The map is not the territory

The meaning of the communication is the response it elicits

You have all the resources to do whatever you want to do

There is a positive intention behind every behaviour

If someone else can do it you can too

If you always do what you've always done you will always get what you've always got

There is no failure only feedback

As you can see, I type them out, laminate and guillotine them and keep them in an envelope.

If you always do what you've always done then you will always get what you've always got

This is a great place to start, isn't it? What this belief addresses is the premise that if you keep doing something, eventually it will work. This is a trap we can all fall into at one time or another, often without even realising that we are repeating the same pattern. As parents we may be particularly prone to this as we may follow the pattern we used with our first child with child number two and wonder what's wrong when they don't automatically respond in the same way. But our children are different and may each need a different approach. Continuing to repeat the same pattern won't suddenly begin to work. It's us who need to think of another way for that child which will be more appropriate for them.

As teachers, when children don't understand one way you might be explaining a concept, you need to find another way, you can't just repeat the same explanation hoping that the penny will eventually drop.

Many children expect their parents or teachers to change. 'It's all their fault!' is what they'll say. What this pre-supposition says is that if the result (what you get) is not what you want, then it is YOU who has to change.

For many children this is a new way of thinking, a new way of taking responsibility.

Do something different.

If you do something different you will get a different result.

This is an excellent challenge for children. How often do they repeat the same behaviour, get the same result and wish they'd got another one?

I love this expression and use it frequently,

'What would you like to have happen?'

Ask them what they want to happen in the situation and ask them to describe it in detail, even act it out if that helps. If you have a very young child, ask them to draw what they'd like to see happen. Then ask them what they could do differently to make this result a reality. Discuss with them their different options and how likely each one would bring about the outcome they desire.

You may find some resistance. After all, this may be a pattern that's been going on since early childhood. I find using hypnotic embedded commands quite useful here.

'I'm wondering what you could do to change this?'

'I'm curious about what you can do to make this change happen?'

'I'm wondering when you'll find another option in this situation.'

Clean Language is useful here as well, especially using the time sequenced phrases. This enables them to understand what happens in order so they can see the structure of the behaviour.

'...and when you've done something different, what happens next?'

'...and when you do something different before, what happens then?'

'...and that xxxx... tell me about that.'

'...and when x does y.... what happens next?'

An activity I also find useful for this belief of excellence is using Story Cubes. Of course, you can simply get them to tell a story about a sequence of events that keeps recurring that doesn't give them the result they want. However, I find switching to a right-brain activity such as drawing, storytelling or other creative activity helps shift them into a more imaginative frame of mind where they are more open to other options and changing a behaviour pattern. With the Story Cubes, you can ask them to tell you a story of what normally happens and then repeat the exercise telling the story in other ways to get the result they think would work better for them.

If you're doing this in a school, it would make a great drama activity as groups of students create different outcomes for common playground misunderstandings. You could also set it up as an art activity creating different scenarios or ask students to take videos to show this.

I like the idea of writing a letter from the future to their younger self.

'Imagine you have achieved this thing and you are writing a letter or text telling your younger self, your x (their current age) year old self, how great it is to be doing it.'

The idea of future pacing is to get the brain imagining and creating that outcome in the future where it has already happened. It's like mapping your neural pathways ahead of doing the thing you want to do, so they know where they have to go. The science may not be completely correct here, but you get the idea. If you are interested in the science, follow Dr Joe Dispenza who explains it 'with excellence'.

You have the resources to do whatever you want to do

It is natural to question our ability, and children do this most of the time as they are in a constant state of learning. There will always be someone around who is learning at a faster rate, someone who has greater ability in a subject or has greater sporting or social skills, is more creative and so on.

As parents or teachers, carers or coaches, we too compare ourselves with others. Many is the time I've been waiting for one of my children at the school gate and looked on with amazement at how another mum manages to multi-task or look so wonderful just after giving birth. As a coach and writer, I have admired blog posts and articles written by other coaches and been envious of their skills.

But just imagine – what if you had all the resources already?

Children get into the habit of saying 'I can't'. We might 'rescue' as parents or teachers. The pattern continues and you can read all about this in the Drama Triangle chapter.

Sometimes they genuinely can't do it. Yet.

This belief of excellence is all about them having the resources to do it and of course NLP Modelling is key here.

Children can tell you who <u>can</u> do it, so ask them

'Who do you know who can do it?'

They may name someone they know at school or it may be a famous person. Whomever it is, and several models of excellence would be useful, you have a model of excellence which you/they can then model. This is a great resource that they can use time and time again for anything they want to do. How powerful is that?

Remember, too, that they may already have this model of excellence themselves and simply have it in an area of their life that they have separated off, thinking it irrelevant for what they want to do now.

MY SKILL WALL

I am good at	My friends say I am	I feel good when I
	This is a hole. You can get through it by using some of these skills, which will you use?	

Exercise

Explain that this is a brick wall. Each brick represents a skill or collection of skills that enable you to get through the hole in the wall to achieve whatever you want. In each brick they are to write:

o *a skill they have;*

o *one that someone has commented on;*

o *something they must have in order to do the activity in which they are great.*

I usually find that they write activities or hobbies in each box like 'gymnastics' or 'funny' or 'art'. This is fine and it's a great starting point. For each they have written, ask:

'And what's the skill you use for that activity?' or 'When you do that activity, what are the skills you need?'

I then write alongside that box the skills they've mentioned and before long we have quite a few. We are both usually very impressed and they find it surprising to have so many skills when they just thought they were good at that activity.

I like to help them build a 'skill wall'. This is a great exercise to help children break down activities they excel in and enjoy, to discover the underlying skills.

I remember on my NLP Master Practitioner training with Sue Knight that we were asked what we were good at. I pondered for a while and said I was good at doing cartwheels.

It seemed like nothing important and I was slightly embarrassed because after all, can't everyone do a cartwheel? But here's the thing – when we can do a thing well, we find it easy and assume (wrongly) that everyone can do it.

So, interestingly, when you break down the cartwheel activity you get:

o the ability to trust that your one hand can take the weight of the rest of your body, if only for a moment;
o not minding looking a bit mad (unless you're a child of course!);
o being ok upside down;
o finding it fun;
o trusting your body to end up upright.

For me, I acknowledged that this activity showed that I had the skills to trust my ability and accept that I can be different, look at my world from another angle (upside down!) and have fun. In that one activity, so casually mentioned, was who I am.

Who is your client?

Who are you?

What do you do well?

Exercise

What I do well is

The skills I use to do this are:
1.
2.
3.
4.
5.

Having these skills means I can

....

....

Specifically, as a Practitioner/Parent/Teacher, this means I can do these things with excellence:

....

....

As well as these skills, they can model others, learn from other people and from all their experiences. They can practise their skills and persevere until they improve and develop them.

Having the belief that they can do something is key. This is why the modelling process emphasises this stage.

There is no failure only feedback

This is often the belief of excellence that I have most difficulty with, and this says more about me than about the belief – this will be true for you, too, with any beliefs of excellence that you question. What we struggle with will be our learning, as it will be for our children, pupils and clients and that is perhaps why the universe has sent them to us. As coaches we tend to attract those who see us as slightly further along their life journey. We may seem to have life a bit more under control and we are their model for what they seek.

Children and teens tend to say that this belief just isn't true even if it may be a desirable belief. A 'fail' in a test is a 'fail' however you look at it, they tell me. They do have a point in terms of the educational system but it certainly doesn't mean that they have failed because in NLP terms we believe that everyone does the best they can given the resources they have and the situation. Tests, exams, appraisals, reviews – these are all part of life. We are judged both formally and informally whatever we do and wherever we go. As practitioners we may feel that we are judged by how many clients we have, how many articles we have published, how much we earn, how many testimonials or referrals we get. As parents we feel judged by our own parents, our parents-in-law, other parents and perhaps our own children.

But, wait! These are all judgements by others, we are 'external referencing' – taking our self-esteem from the opinion of others. What about how <u>we</u> feel about our own efforts? How well are we aligned to our own values?

Also, remember we cannot control others.

'Control your controllables.'

Focus instead on how <u>you</u> feel about your performance.

As parents we often feel we have failed and this frequently happens because we *delete*. We don't see the whole picture and focus instead on the part that fits our belief, so we notice where things didn't go as we wanted or expected. We delete by missing out the context or the details.

We *generalise* by saying that this <u>always</u> happens, or they <u>never</u> listen.

And we *distort* and make this mean that we are a failure.

Understanding how they have done this, really helps parents understand how they have framed a situation and associated into it. By disassociating and taking the emotion out (hard for us parents) and seeing it in context as only <u>part</u> of the picture, helps them see the bigger picture and get a different perspective. Perhaps one that's more about 'doing the best I could', which is pretty much what we all do, isn't it?

Example

My client, a nine-year-old girl, was struggling with her dad's negativity. She spends 50:50 time with mum and dad. Mum is super positive, but dad is quite negative and critical, which she takes personally, making it mean that he doesn't love her.

I asked her to take three pieces of paper and on the top of one to write 'what's gone well', on the second 'what could be better' and on the third, 'overall what's good'.

We then listed happy times with her dad:

'We couldn't stop laughing over a story.'

'We love dancing to rock music.'

'Dad listened when I read out my story.'

'We love camping together, just the two of us.'

'Cuddles when he kisses me goodnight.'

'Shared favourite movies.'

The idea of listing and focusing on the positive is that it shows clients how to reframe when all they can see is the negative and as a result, they make this mean that in some way they have failed: as a daughter, wife, mum.

We then looked at 'areas for improvement'.

We made another list. This took longer, as my client had to acknowledge that some things were in her control where before she had been simply reacting to him and focusing on his negativity. This was in stark contrast to mum's positivity. But she managed to find some pretty good ideas for her list:

'Make more opportunities to see and talk to him.'

'Use lunchtime as a chance to chat.'

'Ask if I can help make the meal.'

'Get him to help with my drawing and do drawing projects together.'

The last list was more about finding points of connection with her dad that she could focus on, going forward:

'We have the same sense of humour.'

'We are both physical.'

'We are both creative.'

Her mum said she was very uplifted by the session and was looking forward to her next stay with her dad which was a great relief for mum.

It is enormously reassuring for children and teenagers (and indeed parents and adults) to take on board the idea that in every negative experience there is learning.

I explain it to children like this:

'Imagine you're a scientist doing experiments, or an engineer designing something amazing. If every time something didn't work, you gave up, then how will anything new and exciting ever be made? No, as you discover something hasn't worked, think,

o What <u>did</u> work?
o What could I do differently next time?
o What is the overall positive outcome?'

This is called a feedback sandwich.

I like to encourage children to keep a Gratitude Diary so they can record things that have gone well each day. Focusing on the good things before going to sleep really aids a good night's rest which is so important for us all. I also encourage them to journal, and this can be done any time, but is especially good to do after school. This way they can 'dump' anything that hasn't gone well, reflect on it and, by offloading it to their diary, they take some ownership rather than looking to a parent to 'fix' it.

The essence is to extract the positive intention, the benefit. So, even if things look bleak, there is something good there if you look hard enough. You can even inject some humour into the session as together you try to find this positive benefit. Be curious. Encourage your child or client to be curious with you and see what you can discover.

What you want to be teaching them is a different response to criticism or negative experiences. We want them to respond, 'OK so what is the learning here?'

Remember that parents are their model for how to manage feedback and perceived failure, so when you think 'my child copes badly with failure', the question to yourself is, 'how do I manage failure?' This is also true for clients. You will make more headway with the child when you first manage it with Mum or Dad. Suggest a couple of sessions with the main carer and then have a gap for the learning and changes to integrate. Then follow up with child client sessions to see what else needs to be tackled.

As a parent or teacher, how could you share your failures with children?

There are some great videos on failure on YouTube and it's worth mentioning famous people, like J K Rowling, who was rejected some 12 times before she found a publisher for her Harry Potter books. Many successful entrepreneurs did not have a successful school career, and so on. Failure is part of the learning process and sometimes failing in something can lead to an even more successful outcome than you expect.

Exercise

I like to use the Story Cubes for this concept. Perhaps it's because feedback is a bit like telling ourselves a story. By separating ourselves and our own emotions, by disassociating, we can see more clearly how we have deleted, distorted and generalised.

Ask your client to shake the cubes and create a story of someone who turned their failure into a learning.

I would usually ask a client to do this several times in order to really reinforce the changed frame. They can tell different stories of different children in a variety of situations: home, school, sport and so on.

Exercise

Ask your child or teen to draw a picture of something that, for them, was a failure. Ask them to tell you what's happening in the picture.

Now ask them to change the picture so it is no longer a failure picture. Could they add in more information, other people, another perspective? I find it interesting to note the colours used.

Ask them to imagine that they are a CCTV camera looking onto the scene, what can the camera see that they might be missing. When we are emotionally involved we see things in an associated way but there is another way to look at it where we see the full picture, and that includes the learning.

I've heard it said that the best teachers in a subject are those who struggled with it at school because they understand the pitfalls and can be more understanding than a teacher who always found the subject easy.

Learning from failure, or rather 'perceived failure', can be hard and it's certainly harder when children compare themselves with others, which of course they do, as do we. This is called 'external referencing'. If you imagine a continuum with internal referencing at one end and external at the other, I think it's good to encourage children to develop some flexibility (the person with the most flexibility controls the system) so they can move along the line as necessary.

They can learn from those who they think do something better; they are their models of excellence. However, they do also have their own internal model of excellence (we already have all the resources we need) and can use their learning skills to improve on whatever they want. So, I ask child clients 'Who does this thing successfully?' if they talk about failure and then I show them the modelling process so they can benefit from the comparison rather than be intimidated by it.

As practitioners, note that we too can find this concept hard. We all get lean weeks, quiet months. How do we use that time? We could worry and feel a failure or look to see what the successful practitioners do. This quiet spell may be a great opportunity to write some great blog posts, pitch an article or interview to your local paper, make some calls to schools to book a slot to come in and talk about NLP or read some books and articles that will improve your knowledge.

In 2020, when we experienced Covid-19, lockdown and social distancing, our lives and those of families around the world, changed forever. The economy collapsed, house prices fell, people died, but out of that came a greater appreciation of community, family, kindness and the value we placed on the NHS and key workers. Nature flourished and pollution fell.

Every 'failure' holds opportunity. Grab it!

If someone else can do it, you can too, or 'you spot it you've got it'

What we observe in others is usually a reflection of something in us. That's how we recognise it. We might call it our 'shadow'.

If it is a positive thing we've noticed in someone else, this is a reflection of our own quality and it shows us and feeds back to us something we do well, with excellence. The question to encourage your client or child to ask themselves when they mention something like this is:

'And how do you do that?'

Together you can explore the structure of that excellence, get the structure, get the belief, and code it for future use in another area of their life.

But what if it is something negative?

'When we find ourselves noticing someone being a bit mean, talking too loudly, sounding off about something, whatever we notice – in what way do we do that too?'

It's called our *shadow* because it may be a part of us that we aren't too proud of so there will be resistance. We will say 'I don't do that,' but we do, otherwise how would we recognise it and respond in that way? The more intensely we respond, the more in the shadow it is. It is a trigger and needs to be worked on whether for ourselves or our client.

The exercise below is a great way to encourage children to identify their qualities and skills on the basis that the person who most inspires them connects to something in them.

Exercise

Who inspires you?

It could be someone at school, or in the wider world: celebrities, sports heroes, TV characters, it doesn't matter because it's the quality that we're after.

What is the specific quality?

'And where in your life do you also have that quality?'

There will be a place, a time, an occasion. Once you've identified that they also have the quality, ask them,

'Now you've spotted it and you know you've got it, how could you use it more often?'

I remember doing this with an A Level history student who told me that her hero was Joan of Arc. When I asked her what she admired about her, she said that Joan of Arc was brave, fearless, willing to stand up for what she believed in and that she was honest. I asked her how she was like this and she said that she supported her friends even when it might be better not to, she was honest and brave and determined to fight for what she believed to be right in the world.

I love doing this one with teachers as a workshop because they tend to underestimate their skills, and it can be quite moving when they realise their skills have been noticed by their peers.

Exercise

Line up the teachers opposite each other.

Line A tells Line B who inspires them and <u>how</u> they inspire them (the way they...) rather than 'why'.

Line B feedback how they've noticed that characteristic in them 'and I've noticed that in you when you...'

Line A moves one person along.

Line B tells Line A who inspires them and the exercise is repeats for the other person.

The map is not the territory

We are working with children and teens, at least that's my assumption. Unless I'm very much mistaken, you are not a child or teen yourself. You probably have your own children and you probably have nieces and nephews, maybe step-children, and this will give you some insight for sure. This is obviously very helpful but these children are ones with whom there is some connection already and some history. You will have watched them grow up and know a lot about them. You will also share some biological connection and have shared values and personality traits. So whilst you are in a great place to do this work with your experience of children, you have one perception of them that is based on your own map of the world. This is not theirs. Nor will their parent have the same map of their territory or yours.

This belief of excellence is about respecting the fact that how our client perceives their world is their truth. It is how it is. Fact. That's what we are going to be working with, so I like to start there. I have the parent's version and know what he/she thinks is going on but it almost certainly is different for the child.

This is obvious when you consider how your children see their world. Their map is very different from ours. Their priorities are different and based on a very small map, mostly involving them. They have no or very little awareness of the bigger picture that we see, and as parents or teachers we usually want to protect them from this, for a while at least. Children inhabit quite an insular space centred on the home and school plus a small area of community. It is a world where they feel safe and loved, where the worst thing they can think of is that world changing. As I write this, here today in the UK as everywhere in the world, we are in lockdown and most schools are closed with children being home-schooled. Is it any wonder I'm seeing so many children and teens online for anxiety issues? As I write, they have now announced that children may have to wear masks at school and it is reported that a great many parents and teachers are saying that this will be a huge issue for children with Autism and ADHD.

Children fear change because so much is still unknown to them and they have no experience of it to reassure them that they will be OK. When we encounter change we usually have something similar that we can draw on for reassurance and to give us confidence. We can usually help children cope with change in the same way, although right now we are all in a strange and unfamiliar world, so we aren't able to reassure our children as we might normally, as we don't know ourselves what will happen. We can't answer their many questions and this in itself gives them anxiety as we are supposed to be the ones to know.

In the first parent and child appointment of 90 minutes I nearly always ask the child or teen to create their world using a sand tray. You may think this a bit babyish for a teen, but after the initial surprise at seeing it on the table in a therapy room (or outside, which is where we've had to be to ensure social distancing lately) when they had been expecting a more formal setup, they get stuck in and totally enjoy themselves. Remember that the language of the subconscious is colour and image. Sand play is an Art Therapy technique that I find clients love, young and old, and it has the unique ability to be constantly tweaked – added to, changed, taken away from – in much the same way as we alter our own perceptions as we process our experience. In that way, it is unlike a drawing in that once a drawing is drawn, it is difficult to change without spoiling it (for the client I mean). They usually want to do the drawing again. Whereas what we observe with the sand tray is that we can watch what they change and later ask them about it.

> 'The language of visual art – colours, shapes, lines and images – speaks to us in ways that words cannot. Art Therapy is a modality that uses the nonverbal language of art for personal growth, insight, and transformation and is a means of connecting what is inside us – our thoughts, feelings, and perceptions – with outer realities and life experiences. It is based on the belief that images can help us understand who we are and enhance life through self-expression.'
>
> *(Taken from the Introduction of*
> *'The Art Therapy Sourcebook' by Cathy A Malchiodi)*

I have an amazing inflatable tray and some lovely pink sand. Then I have Tupperware containers of dinosaurs, shells, sea creatures, Moshi monsters, LEGO figures and various other things that I might add to the collection. I've just bought a set of colour cards and I may add those in. This is one of the very few exercises that I haven't successfully been able to replicate online.

I take a photo for my records and invite them to take one for themselves.

I do usually go on to create their compelling outcome for their world but that belongs in a different chapter. For now we are focusing on how they perceive their world as it is.

It's about perceptions. We all have different perceptions of our environment depending on our age, life stage, culture and experiences. To assume our perceptions are the only correct ones would be unecological in NLP terms.

Exercise

'I'd like you to create your world in this sand tray. Include whatever is in your world, your home, other homes you spend a lot of time in, your school and activities that are really important to you. Make sure you put in yourself and all those special people in your life.'

I then stay silent, observing. I watch what changes they make, what pauses and questions they ask. It's interesting to pick up their metaprogrammes. Are they seeking detail, anxious to 'get it right', do they keep refining and changing even after they seem to have finished? How they do this exercise is how they do 'life'. It is their pattern. Note anything you want to ask afterwards.

When they've stopped tweaking and tell you they've finished ask:

'Tell me about your world.'

Notice where they start and use 'clean questions' all the time to explore colour, positioning, metaphors, choice of animal or shell, size, proportion and so on. Avoid using the 'why' word, instead ask:

'Tell me about this.'

'What is there about that?'

'What does the colour mean to you?'

'... and that's like...?'

You can add your own questions as well at the end.

Also ask about anything that you might have expected to be there but isn't such as a missing parent or sibling.

There is a positive intention behind every behaviour

This belief of excellence can be hard for us to accept when there is so much evil in the world and so many dangers for children. But there always has been. Perhaps now the dangers are simply different. Those who would harm the people we love are what we would call Persecutors in the Drama Triangle but when you read that chapter, you will learn that they have moved into that role from the role of Victim. Before they lashed out, they felt like the victim in their life. They couldn't stand it anymore and, because their model was violent, that was the only response they knew. Children are not born bad or violent. They learn it from the people around them as they grow up.

This belief is similar in many ways to 'there's no failure, only feedback' because it encourages us to look for the learning and move on. It shows us that there is another perspective in the situation and when we step away from our own viewpoint, and look at it from a more impartial perspective, 'the computer' as Virginia Satir would say, we find that there is something we've missed.

Behind every behaviour there is something positive and it is our job to find it.

Example

I had a teenage client who was referred to me because she was repeatedly sick and the doctor could find nothing wrong.

It can be useful to find out when a particular feeling started, in this case the feeling of being sick. I wanted to find out whether that was the first time?

She described to me being in the classroom for a lesson taught by a supply teacher. The other girls were messing around very obviously, quite rudely (she felt), and the supply teacher was struggling to cope and was getting flustered. My client felt uncomfortable for her, embarrassed for her friends and a bit sick.

She put her hand up and asked to be excused to go to the toilet. She was immediately sent to the medical room and her mum was called to collect her. They went home and had a lovely afternoon together watching a movie on TV and eating chocolates (yes, I know!).

Anyway, this situation continued with more frequent episodes of 'sickness' unrelated to the first incident. I say 'sickness' because in fact she was never actually physically sick.

I introduced my client to the idea that there is a positive intention behind every behaviour and invited her to consider what hers was. 'I have no idea,' she said, and it did seem to be genuine bewilderment.

'Be curious.'

Still nothing.

So I ventured, 'I think if I got to have my mum all to myself for an afternoon watching TV rather than being at school, I might think this was a positive benefit.'

She nodded.

She then went on to explain that her mum worked full time and she had a sister with cerebral palsy who attended a different school and was brought home by taxi. The taxi arrived about the same time as she did which meant that when she got home, her mother was fully occupied with her sister and she just had to do her homework and then help prepare the meal. Her mum then put her sister to bed and then she went to bed on her own, so there was no time for her to have her mother to herself at all. She loved her sister and fully understood the situation, and she wouldn't even want to change it, but she felt sad that she didn't have any time with her mum just as she was becoming a teenager and wanted to talk to her.

I asked her if she could ask her mum for some time together but she didn't want to put any more pressure on her mum than she already had. I suggested that her mum was obviously worried about her daughter's sickness so she needed to explain and tell her what she needed, leaving mum to answer for herself rather than assuming the answer.

When her mum came to collect her, she asked her for some 'together-time'. Her mum started saying "But you know I…" and the daughter looked at me, I looked at her mum and she realised this was important. 'Maybe I can ask Sheila next door to sit with Beatrice on a Saturday morning and we can go shopping, have a coffee and a chat?' My client glowed with happiness.

Expressing our needs when we are in victim mode and when we feel helpless is the best way to step away and take responsibility for our needs, and this also applies to those who do us harm. They too have unmet needs and understanding them and finding the positive intent will help us have healthier connections.

The question to ask is, 'When I do the behaviour I'm observing, what is my positive intention, could this be true for them?'

You cannot not communicate

This belief is about how we cannot <u>not</u> communicate. How we choose to sit, stand, hold ourselves, where we look, our facial expressions, everything about us and our environment, our clothes, our home tells a story. This is, of course, true for us as parents, teachers, colleagues and as practitioners.

Many parents tell me, 'we haven't told the children,' or, 'he doesn't know', 'we've told him it doesn't matter,' – but you are like cling film. Your child is a part of you and will pick up your feelings as if they were their own. This has been so true during Covid-19. Children have been telling me that they're worried a parent will get the virus, be ill, possibly die, lose their job, split up and other worries about grandparents. They know their parents are worried so rather than share these thoughts and feelings with them, they bottle them up and I've been seeing a lot of clients with eating disorders, toilet problems, and so on. This has been partly exacerbated by parents telling them that everything is OK and they have nothing to worry about when the children can hear their parents arguing, shouting at them and crying. They pick up the atmosphere because they are part of you.

So, how is this relevant when working with children?

Whilst children pick up the energy from their parents, they are usually blissfully unaware of how they project their own. I've had numerous children complain they have no friends, and yet when they act out how they go into school and how they are in the playground, or how they do a drawing, it's clear that they are creating a huge barrier to friendship just by how they present themselves.

What you put out there is what you attract.

Example

I had an interesting discussion with one girl who had described dragging herself up the path to the playground, sitting on a bench, head downcast, wondering why no-one would come and sit with her.

When she did this exercise, she said, 'I didn't realise how grumpy I looked. No wonder no-one wanted to sit with me, I look scary,' and of course this was not the case.

23

Exercise

Ask your client to think about not having any friends and feeling sad about it – as they've just described.

Ask what colour they feel or what animal. It's great for children to use metaphors to capture their state. It comes easily to them, easier than words.

Ask them how likely they are to attract a friend in this state. Yes or No?

Ask them to rate their state 0-10 with 10 being super happy and 0 being very sad.

Take a photo of them.

Do a 'break state'. You can do a little dance or wiggle or sighing, whatever you usually do as a 'break state' exercise. The idea is to change from the state they're in and create a different one. Any way that abruptly alters the breath will work.

Now ask them to think about being the most popular child in the school, how does that feel? Imagine they have loads of friends, everyone's waving and smiling at them and they are happy to be there, looking forward to their day at school.

What's the colour? What animal?

How likely are they to attract a friend now?

Rate their state again 0-10 and take a photo of them.

Compare the photos, compare the state ratings and the likelihood of attracting a friend.

You'll find you don't need to say anything. It will be really obvious to them that what they think and feel is communicated to their physiology and this is picked up by everyone around them. Make sure to delete the photos of course!

Everything we say and do, and the way we do it, is a communication that gets a response, so it's important to take responsibility for your intentions. If the response isn't what you expected, then change the communication.

Working with children, it is so important that we communicate what we want, which, in my case is: approachable, accepting/non-judgemental, kind (but not gullible), adult rather than parent or friend, flexible, curious, patient. I do this by being me, rather than putting on a professional persona, and by using a table with plenty of fun stuff on it, sand play, LEGO, felt pens and paper, Story Cubes, etc. I wear slippers and casual clothes but I'm meticulous about punctuality and the room is always prepared for the next client so they can see I'm looking forward to seeing them. How you communicate who you are and what you offer and expect is up to you but it needs to be considered.

With the best will in the world we sometimes find that we have not communicated what we intended, either personally or with our client or their parent. When this happens, we need to take responsibility and ask if we can reword it to express what we intended. I do this with clients too. If I'm not sure what they intend to communicate I ask,

'That sounded like... is that what you meant to communicate?'

It can happen sometimes when you get close to uncovering something significant and they might shrug their shoulders, look down or say, 'don't know'.

Silence communicates. It communicates trust, acceptance, patience, willingness to listen and hold the space and expectation that something will be said or drawn.

A good rule of thumb is to think before communicating. Think about your compelling outcome and consider the person with whom you're communicating, how will they best receive the communication? The VAK and metaprogramme chapter will be really helpful with this, in order to maximise rapport.

The person with the most flexibility influences the outcome of any interaction

I love this one! It is perfect for children because it is all about new possibilities and that can be fun. It's about changes and choices. I often introduce them to this concept by saying,

'Imagine on your computer keyboard you only had one key and that's all you could use? Or on your piano keyboard you could only use one key? How could you create a beautiful story or a beautiful piece of music with just one key or one note? Use the whole keyboard and combine that with your curiosity to explore how you can use the full capability of that keyboard and you will make beautiful music or a beautiful story.'

Children often feel that they don't have many choices, their life is controlled by parents and teachers, sometimes also older siblings and even younger siblings who take priority. Their choice can be binary: yes or no, this way or that way, your way or my way. But there are, in fact, many ways and children have the imagination to explore them, but usually don't because they feel powerless to do so.

Example

James hated his name. His friends at school teased him calling him 'Jamie' singing 'Jamie, Jamie, Jamie,' which really annoyed him. It annoyed him so much that he would punch whoever he could reach. He was told off, Mum was called into the school and he was told not to do it again. He tried walking away but this made it worse because the boys chased after him. He tried ignoring it but he couldn't.

I put a wastepaper basket in the middle of the room and gave him a tennis ball.

'How many different ways can you get that tennis ball in the basket?' I asked him.

He was nine years old so I suggested that nine was a good number to aim for.

James had great fun doing this. I find if you can create a physical task for children to get the learning, it works much better than simply telling them.

Once he'd done that, I put out a big sheet of paper and gave him some felt pens.

'Now write down nine ways you can respond differently to your friends when they tease you.'

He spent some time thinking about it and managed nine ways. Not all of them would have been successful in my opinion but remember 'the map is not the territory'. What do I know about the world of nine-year-olds in the playground? I only know what I'm told, not how it actually is.

I feel much of our work is to encourage children to build this flexibility muscle and gain the power of choice in their life through understanding how their mind works, their filters, and how to access different language patterns to gain rapport then pace to lead. It is often when children feel metaphorically 'backed into a corner' that they fight back, often with unintended consequences.

The point of the exercise is much more about a child taking responsibility for their response, taking control and having other choices available to control the situation for themselves.

The more choices you have, the greater flexibility you have.

Other ways we can limit our choices is by using 'stuck' words like 'must', 'should', 'ought to' rather than 'unstuck' words like 'could'.

Here, instead of doing what we'd like to do, we do what we 'should' do.

'I'd love to go for a walk in nature but I must do the shopping.'

Of course, there are things we do have to do, but again, are there ways to create choice or at least the sense of choice?

'I'm going to go for a walk in nature and then go shopping.'

We also have the choice of being in rapport or not, knowing how we communicate, whether we tend to use visual, auditory or kinaesthetic language patterns and which metaprogrammes we use. So when our communication isn't working as we'd like, we can switch to another.

Having flexibility as a practitioner is so important. We see children of all ages and with different ways of processing their world, different experiences and different levels of emotional intelligence and verbal skills. By having access to a wealth of activities, ideas and techniques, we can find the best way to connect with each child and help them achieve the learning they need.

The mind and body are one

Your mind and your body are connected; they are one. When you don't feel well, when you are in pain, it will affect your emotions. You might feel sad, frustrated, annoyed. When we feel well and healthy, we feel happy and content with life. There is actually a biological reaction that takes place too.

In Dr David Hamilton's book 'The 5 side effects of kindness' he explains that when we are kind or experience warm emotions, we produce endorphins which are often called the 'happy hormones' which tell our mind that we are happy. These endorphins increase oxytocin which in turn releases the chemical nitric oxide. This expands the blood vessels thereby reducing blood pressure.

I love to introduce children to some simple exercises to show them how their mind and body are connected.

Exercise

Ask them to hold their non-dominant arm out at the side of their body.

Tell them you are just going to push it down. They do not need to resist. It's not a strength test. This is just to give you a sense of what resistance would be there normally, a control, if you like.

Then let them return their arm to where it was.

Now ask them to think about a really happy time, getting a good mark or making a new friend.

Push their arm down. They will be much stronger.

They return their arm to the starting point.

Now ask them to think about something a bit sad such as getting a bad mark or mum telling them off.

Push their arm down. You'll find it much easier to do.

The arm is the same, your pressure is just the same – the only difference is their thoughts.

Here's another one that does not require a helper so it's probably better for a classroom.

Exercise

Ask them to hold their arm out in front of them, straight ahead with their finger pointed.

Ask them to now take their arm to the side and as far behind them as they can. They should notice what their finger is pointing at.

Then ask them to return their arm to the starting position.

This time ask them to imagine getting it further round when they move it.

How much further can they go?

They can return their arm to the front again.

Now ask them to be really curious and say 'I'm wondering how much further you can go?'

They do this again.

How many had found they could get their arm much further round when they used their mind as well?

The 'I'm wondering' is a hypnotic embedded command and is very effective for encouraging children (or adults) to go further and do more than they previously thought possible.

These exercises lead very naturally into a discussion of how they may currently be letting their mind influence their body or vice versa.

You know how it is when you are 'in flow'? Everything is going well, we feel great and it shows in our body, our breathing and our state of mind. This is because they are all connected.

Then, maybe something goes wrong, a client or a parent is late or you have to pick the kids up from school and you can't park and... we are no longer 'in flow', our breathing is faster, we are edgy and our body feels stiff and our words more stilted.

It's like that for children too. They are angry and they make fists and cry and shout and their whole body tells you they are not happy.

Show children how they can change their physiology to change their state. As children play with showing their emotions in their body and vice versa, you are helping them to build emotional intelligence.

The fastest way to change your state is to move your body. Here are some great ways to teach this concept to kids.

1. Movement

Simply by moving, we increase the oxygen flow to our brain and the rest of our body, we see new and different things and create new possibilities.

- o Look up (connects with the visual part of our brain, images of possibilities).
- o Walk or run about so you breathe faster.
- o Yoga encourages deeper breathing throughout the body and stills the busy mind.
- o Walk in nature, the fresh air and the stillness together with the walking motion will be calming.

2. Laughter

Laughter has a huge number of psychological benefits relieving pain and stress and increasing immunity. It reduces the stress hormones: cortisol, epinephrine (adrenaline), dopamine and growth hormone and it increases endorphins. It also increases the number of antibody-producing cells creating a stronger immune system.

Laughter provides a physical and emotional release and a good belly laugh exercises the diaphragm, contracts the abs and even works out the shoulders leaving muscles more relaxed.

It distracts us from negative emotions in a more beneficial way than other distractions and gives us a light-hearted perspective.

Good ways to get laughing are to watch comedy, tell jokes or... wait for it... have a good fake belly laugh. How does this work? Because your brain does not know the difference.

Yes, you can get just the same stress relief from a fake laugh. Fake it until you make it.

I've shown this to many clients.

Exercise

'How happy do you feel right now on a scale of 1-10, 1 being really sad and 10 being super happy?'

Most clients will choose some figure around 4-6.

'Now I want you to imagine something really funny you've seen in a movie. See it, hear it, feel it as if you're watching it right now.'

Pause.

'Now I want you to give a huge belly laugh.'

'Can you tell me how happy you are on that 1-10 scale?'

It will be a lot higher.

They can do this for themselves by:

- o *seeing the funny side of something;*
- o *reframing it as funny;*
- o *distract themselves by thinking of something funny;*
- o *or just by randomly laughing.*

Laughter really is the best medicine.

3. Mindfulness

Mindfulness reduces stress and decreases anxiety, making it an excellent tool for us to share with our clients, children and for us to use ourselves. Check out the chapter on Mindfulness later in the book.

Your mental state affects your physiology and vice versa. How you 'show up', your physiology, expresses what's going on in your mind. What you're thinking affects how you look, what you can do physically. You can change your state by changing your physiology especially through changing your breathing. Hence why yoga, mindfulness, meditation, laughter, exercise and so on, really cheer us up, calm us down, relax us and change our state in a resourceful way.

4. Yoga

There are many different types of yoga practice, some involving heat, others include chanting or meditation but they all connect your mind and body through intentional breathing. Deep breathing is an effective way to reduce stress because it sends a message to your brain to calm down by telling it that you are already calm. We can trick the brain by 'faking it' as we 'make it' as we did with the laughter exercise.

In yoga we can deepen poses through 'breathing into the muscle' reassuring it that it can move a bit more. Sometimes muscles can tense to protect us from hurting ourselves even when there is no potential threat. By breathing deeply into the muscle, it will relax and let you find that deeper pose.

5. Meditation

There are different types of meditation and many schools include a meditation in their day to calm children at registration and after lunch break so they can find their best learning state. Meditations can be self-guided or you can download meditations. There are a number of great ones specifically for children and for specific issues such as nightmares, sleep, bed-wetting, anxiety and so on.

6. EFT

Emotional Freedom Technique involves tapping on the meridian lines of the body which connect to specific organs. The tapping, either silent or using the child's words, connects mind and body and it is effective for a great many conditions such as pain, grief, anger, anxiety and low self-esteem. More in the EFT chapter.

(2)

FOCUSING ON THE POSITIVE OUTCOME

SETTING COMPELLING OUTCOMES AND IDENTIFYING SKILLS AND QUALITIES. ANCHORING AND CIRCLE OF EXCELLENCE

It's tempting to say that every chapter of this book should provide enough material for teachers and coaches for use in workshops, with one-to-one clients and in family sessions, but surely what all therapy, particularly NLP and EFT, have in common is to elicit and work on your client's compelling outcomes. As a parent this will be your overriding mission as well, of course, as for your children.

I'm often asked how important the parent's 'compelling outcome' is. I would say that it's of interest but whilst it may be compelling for the parent or the teacher, social worker or similar, it's unlikely to be compelling for the child. Over the years, I've learnt that when we meet the child's compelling outcome, we also meet that of the parent and teacher. Let me explain: say the child's compelling outcome is to score more goals, make more friends as they know this will make them happy and feel confident, have more self-belief, want to get up in the morning, and feel positive. These are what will enable them also to work harder in lessons and behave better or whatever the parent or teacher wants. So I ask you, parents, to set aside your own goals for your children and help them meet their own. Then, watch and observe how your own goals for them are met as they grow in confidence through having met what makes them happy. Children are not going to engage in a process that will require some emotional work unless they are invested in the outcome.

NLP is all about patterns and beliefs of excellence. So, whatever compelling outcome we end up working on with our child, there will be transferable skills and beliefs into the world of education.

Example

A mum wanted her son to see me to gain skills he could use in maths. On the day, his mum called to say he wouldn't come. It wasn't too surprising, since it clearly wasn't his compelling outcome. I asked if he'd come if we played football outside in the garden. He was fine with that and arrived in football kit, with his football, and we played. I love using my outside space. Who said therapy has to happen in a room?

He was clearly a very skilled player. I asked him to show me how to do some of his tricks with the ball. I observed how meticulously he explained the steps, the process and how patient he was with me, being gentle in correcting my mistakes and repeatedly showing me the bit I was getting wrong. We built great rapport and soon I was able to dig deeper to get his underlying belief. Yes, this was a modelling session! Believe that your client has all the resources he needs as per the NLP beliefs of excellence, and trust the process, trust your own skills and intuition. By getting to the underlying belief behind his ability to do these tricks or 'skills' as he called them, we found his belief of excellence and guided him to move that across to other areas of his life.

So, my questions were modelling ones.

'How do you do that?'

Copy the steps and the structure until you get the process.

What is your belief in that moment?

He says, 'I want to get past the opposition.'

And what is your belief about yourself? I explain that we call this 'a belief of excellence' which I can see really appeals to him!

'I have lots of skills and I know which one will be best in each situation.' Then he added: *'And if it isn't, I use a different one.'*

We then discussed how football <u>might be</u> a metaphor. I explain what a metaphor is and ask:

'If getting past the opposition was a metaphor, what might it be similar to?'

He said, *'Overcoming problems... like in Maths!'*

It's always going to be more compelling when they make the discovery themselves.

'And the skills?' I ask.

'They are like Maths skills. I know different ways to do Maths questions so I could think about which is the best for that question, like in my football.'

'And the belief of excellence?' I continue.

'That I have the skills and if I get it wrong, I have other skills I can try.'

We then did a quick anchoring exercise to make the association readily available by creating an anchor that he could use in class. He chose to make a ball shape with his right thumb and index finger to remind him of football.

Note that I don't <u>tell</u>, I try and <u>show</u>, so they complete the learning piece of the exercise themselves.

In that way, Mum's compelling outcome was met through meeting the child's compelling outcome of playing football rather than talking about Maths.

Modelling is a very good way to help children achieve their compelling outcome and I've used it many, many times to help children with social skills and confidence, but it would usually be within a specific session, probably the first in the series of four or six, when we sit down specifically to discuss what the child wants. I set this up by first introducing 'towards' and 'away from' thinking as a concept so they understand how they are different because so many children have been told, time and again what they should 'not do' or what the 'teacher doesn't want to hear or see', 'what Mum and Dad don't want happening again.' So they are expecting to be focusing on reducing unwanted behaviour which is totally 'away from'. Instead I want them to be thinking about what they DO want.

Here's the type of explanation I give but, obviously, you can come up with your own examples.

One of the NLP Meta Programmes is 'towards' and 'away from' thinking. In NLP we like to be solution focused which is 'towards thinking' rather than focusing on the problem which is called 'away from' thinking.

For example:

1) When you do your homework is it because you want to do well at school, please the teacher and get a good mark, or because if you don't you'll be in trouble? (The first is towards and the second is away from.)

2) When you do something new do you think about how well it will go or how much fun it will be? Or do you worry that things might go wrong? (Again, the first is towards, the second is away from.)

I then give them this example, although I have a variety of examples to suit different ages and interests, so just adapt and come up with your own.

'Imagine you've got a netball match against your rival school. They beat you 20-1 last time and you see, as they arrive on court, that they've got their best Goal Shooter playing and she immediately goes to the net during warm up and gets five goals. You think "Oh no, we're going to be beaten again!"'

This is 'away from' thinking. We are focusing on what we don't want to happen and when we do that our brain just hears that this is what will happen. And it does.

The child will recognise this pattern and agree.

But what if you were to think in a 'towards' way, what might you think instead?

The child will suggest:

'This time we're going to win!'
Or decide on something similar which will set the brain thinking
positively. This is how it works best and you will play much better like
that and maybe win. Remember you control your thoughts. We want
our child clients to learn that they have choices. I explain it like this:

Our thoughts are like a keyboard, there are lots of options of what keys to press. You don't just have one choice. The different keys or notes can form beautiful words or pieces of music. Children have an amazing imagination; let them reflect and decide the best belief for the situation. This is not your job. Your job is to provide the safe space to enable them to freely explore that keyboard using their own map of the world knowing you will listen without judgement.

Setting positive, towards-type goals will yield great results because the brain understands positive instruction. It wants to know what you want, not what you don't want. Here's a good quote and one I use very frequently!

Don't think about a pink elephant!
What do you immediately think about?

Obviously, you think about a pink elephant because, in order to follow the instruction, the brain has to conjure up what it is that you *aren't* to think about. Then the deed is done. It's the same thing with setting compelling outcomes. When we think about what we don't want – not having friends, no-one to play with in the playground, the teacher being cross with us, Mum and Dad stopping us from using our phone, we have already created that possibility in our mind.

It is the same for you as a practitioner, set an outcome that looks like this – I don't want to have no clients, I don't want to be short of money, I don't want to get it wrong... and you will not achieve the success in business that you desire. Instead set goals such as:

o Having a full diary of appointments
o Having plenty of money to pay your bills and go on holiday

o Getting loads of referrals
o Being talked about as getting great results with kids
o Being asked to speak at events
o Being asked to run programmes in schools

Teachers, what do you want for your class?

Parents, what would a good outcome look, sound or feel like?

So, if you recognise yourself doing this, you need to ask: 'OK so I know what I don't want but what do I want instead?'

What you're looking for is *the difference that will make the difference.*

Example

A mum came to see me because she was really tired. Her seven-year-old daughter was coming into her room every night and getting into their bed. Her husband slept through it but she couldn't and ended up having to sleep on the floor or going to sleep in her daughter's bed.

'I don't know what to do!' she wailed. 'Every night I tell her "DO NOT come into my room!"'

Well, I'm sure you realise that this is the pink elephant situation again. The little girl is hearing 'come into my room' partly because the brain filters out the 'not' and partly because that's become the pattern.

'If you always do what you've always done, you always get what you've always got," I said, looking meaningfully at her.

She was just so tired and frustrated that she looked at me with no understanding at all.

'I don't know what you mean, I keep telling her not to come into my room, and every night she does.'

So I gently asked her, 'And does this work?'

'No.'

'So what could you do differently?' I ventured, hoping she would realise how using the word 'don't' wasn't helpful.

But instead she started talking about locking the door, putting oil on the handle and other fairly crazy options.

I needed to be more direct, and you will find that you need to be more direct too sometimes. When parents get stuck in a pattern, even though it patently isn't working, they find it impossible to come up with other ideas, unlike children, whose minds are much more flexible and creative.

So, I helped her by using the phrase I mentioned earlier.

'OK, so I know what you don't want but what do you want instead?'

Believe it or not she repeated herself.

'I DON'T WANT HER TO COME INTO MY ROOM!'

She was getting a bit annoyed with me by now so I said, 'What other things could you say? What positive thing do you want her to do? Where should she be?'

Ah! At last, she realised what I meant, and even as she said, 'I could tell her to... stay... in her room...' there was something unfamiliar and strange as if she'd never even thought of asking her to do this.

Anyway, the next morning I had a lovely email thanking me and saying that yes, her daughter had stayed in her room that night.

So, let's crack on with the work you will do with your client or your child on compelling outcomes.

Exercise

Give them paper and felt pens and ask them to write down what they want. I usually suggest that it's like a Christmas present list but not of things like Xbox but wishes for them personally. If they seem unsure, I usually give them an example such as: 'My wish for this session is that you get a better understanding of how your mind works so you have more choices.' So it's pretty clear we're not talking about iPads and iPhones here.

I like to use colour felt pens because colour is the language of the unconscious mind. I don't want a list of goals such as they might be asked to do at school. I want them to dig deeper than that. I want them to be bold and imaginative, positive and greedy for what they want with no holding back and no being sensible.

You will get the odd desired outcome that will not be possible such as 'Mum and Dad getting back together', or 'Granny coming back to life'.

Leave them to write down whatever they choose initially because there will be learning as you go through them together.

Ideally, you need 3 or 4 to work on, but I've had children write down one word or sentence, and I've had some write long lists. If they just can't think of anything, a good option is to ask, 'If your best friend was writing such a list, what would they write?' This way they can project which may feel safer initially.

Now you have a list.

Step 1. Check which ones on their list they can control.

'Control your controllables' is a favourite saying of mine. I think I stole it from my eldest daughter. It's proved very useful in therapy and I've written lots of blog posts on this subject.

So, we question whether each of their wishes passes this test of 'Can I control this?' If it doesn't pass then you ask 'What part of this CAN you control?' This is about controlling their own reaction or response to the situation so you can together reword the wish such that it is in their control.

'I don't want Mrs P to be my teacher next year' becomes 'I want to be OK about Mrs P being my teacher next year.'

'I want Josh to stop bullying me' becomes 'I want to find a way to show Josh that what he's doing is not OK.'

This reframing exercise you'll do with them is an important part of their learning that they have choices, they have power to choose their response.

Step 2. Is it worded as a 'towards' outcome?

Despite explaining the difference between 'towards' and 'away from' at the beginning of the session, I still get children writing 'I don't want to be anxious about tests' or 'I don't want x to be mean to me'.

I remind them about compelling outcomes needing to be worded as what they DO want and then ask them to reword them. Interestingly, I've observed that even in the rewording, something shifts as they reframe internally and realise what it is they want. I urge you to be patient during this rewording and hold back from helping because this stage is important for them to focus on what exactly it is that they want.

Step 3. Applying the SMART criteria.

In the business world, SMART goals are set as a way to be precise about what the team is working towards. It's what we are doing here and it is a discipline that will be helpful to children at school as well. It's basically, in NLP terms, what we might call 'chunking down'. Here we are doing it with intent to create some truly compelling outcomes. This is different to how we might usually 'chunk down' in a session with a client for clarity.

    SMART is the mnemonic for Specific, Measurable, Achievable, Relevant and Time- bound.

    One by one we work through each of the phrases on their wish list and check that they meet these criteria. I tell you now – they won't!

    Why? Because children are not business people and these are things they want personally and come from the heart, not the head, so this is as it should be. It is in the exercise of going through the SMART process that they start making these wishes more conscious and actionable, applying the skills they have to meeting their outcomes. It is a process that draws in the outcome towards them, making it a part of them as they own the process of meeting the outcome rather than just dreaming about it as a distant possibility.

Exercise

Taking their first compelling outcome ask

S – Specific

'What, specifically, do you want?'

I might explain that we call this 'chunking down' in NLP terms because it's a useful process and one that we're likely to be referring to again in a session so why not introduce it now?

For example – 'I want to have more friends' may be their sentence

I would point out that 'more' is what we call 'big chunk' we need 'small chunk' so how many friends exactly do they want?

Now this is often an interesting question because I ask them how many friends they have now and they will typically count them off on their fingers. This may actually be a surprise to them. They realise that they have more than they thought. Maybe it was just a perception that they didn't have many. Now, of course, a perception is their truth but then I ask them, 'who else do you want as a friend so you can have more friends?' They think for a bit, name a few others and usually realise that in fact they are already a friend. This does not always happen and perhaps more with boys than with girls, there may be one or two even who they do want to befriend. We write these names down.

M – Measurable

'How will you know when you've done it?'

In the previous example relating to friends, we might discuss how they will know that this or that child is now a friend. What is a friend? Is it someone who smiles at them in the playground, talks to them, invites them on a playdate, includes them in their game? This is an important and interesting conversation and one that engages their emotional intelligence, self-esteem and social skills.

We will usually come up with some criteria and signs to help them identify who their friends are so they will know when this outcome has been met.

A – Achievable
'Is it possible for you to do this?'

In almost every case I've found that their outcome is possible, and they can see that it is but, nevertheless, the process of them considering whether it is or is not possible is an important one.

One of the reasons that they will agree that it is possible is because we have by now chunked down to the specifics and worked out what they are looking for in terms of signs of friendship. When we start to imagine a thing in that detail we are actually halfway to achieving it, because our brain is creating images and future scenarios which are preparing it for this to happen – and therefore it's possible.

R – Relevant
'How relevant is it to you, will it make a difference in your life?'

Now we get to the crux of the matter. Does it actually matter? Will it make a difference in their life? This is the 'compelling' part of a compelling outcome. Is it just 'nice to have' or is it life changing for them?

Are other wishes more important? If they are then this is a good time to change tack and work on another outcome. It may also be the point where they realise that the outcome they're working on is a parent or teacher's and not theirs but, as I've said, it all works out in the end.

T – Time bound
'When will you do this?'

When are they going to do this? Is it something that 'at some point in the future, maybe next term' they will think about?

In truth, if it's something compelling, they are likely to say 'Monday when I go into school' or 'next playtime' or 'next Maths lesson'.

Step 4. Associating into the compelling outcome

Having treated every item on their 'wish list' to the SMART criteria, having checked that they are controllable and 'towards' I then ask my client to give each one a score out of 10 to reflect how much they want *it. Be prepared for them to give each one a 10/10. Some will even be scored 11. But I pre-frame the question by saying that today we will work on the highest-scoring one, and come back to other high-scoring outcomes in subsequent sessions. If there are several scoring the same, I ask them to choose which they'd like to work on and we fold over the paper so they are only looking at that one, rather than being distracted by other options.*

Now take the highest-scoring one and work with it.

Ask:

a) *What do you want exactly and what will it look/sound/feel like?*

Here we are getting even more 'small chunk' and associating into it visually, auditorily and kinaesthetically. I introduce the 'eye accessing' exercise and ask them to look up to the right and imagine their outcome (now worded to embrace the SMART criteria) and what they will see in the future when it is achieved, what they will hear and what they will feel.

This is future pacing, imagining ourselves in the future with the outcome met. It can be a powerful experience and one that will make an impact on your child client because you're really integrating the outcome in the present.

b) *What will be different when you have it?*

Having briefly visited their future self with the outcome in place and associating into the feeling, they are ready and able to talk about how achieving this outcome will make a difference in their life.

Encourage them to use the words 'I will..." rather than 'I would...' because 'I will' is about future fact rather than future possibility.

c) *What problems could there be when you have it?*

We need to check for resistance. Right now, there may be no problems at all but when they think about what the ramifications might be at school or at home when they achieve their outcome, things may be different and we need to prepare them for this.

d) Why do you want it <u>now</u>?

Is this outcome something that they want one day or next term? Hopefully it's not, as we covered this already in the SMART exercise (if you remember T was time-bound), but things shift a bit as we start to associate and chunk down to the reality of what achieving this outcome will mean for them. It is our job (I believe) to make sure they are 100% committed to it and want it right now.

e) What can you do to get it? What skills do you already have that will help you get it?

This is a meaty section of this process and one that creates a huge shift towards achieving their outcome because they realise that they already have all the resources they need as per the NLP beliefs of excellence. I find it amazing that even though those beliefs were written 60 years ago by two young men, that they remain relevant to families today.

I like to get children writing and drawing wherever possible so this is a great opportunity for another list.

'OK so let's list all the skills you need to achieve this outcome and then we'll tick them off.'

Note my language pattern. I'm assuming the child client already has all the resources they need and I would say that this belief, along with the other NLP beliefs of excellence, really permeates all I do with clients and hopefully in my normal life (whatever that is).

Now children will get stuck into this by writing a list of all the things they are good at but what we want is the skill, so here's what I do:

Exercise

Show them the skill wall I referred to earlier.

'This is your skill wall. Imagine that your compelling outcome is the other side of that wall, through the hole. You need to gather all the skills you need to get through the wall so write in each box something you have – a quality, skill, talent – that in some way will help you achieve your outcome.'

They will probably write the activities or sports they are good at so let them get on with it and fill each brick.

When they have done this, go back through each one and ask:

'You've written football here, what skills do you have in football?'

I find I need to keep pressing so you will need some different prompts here

'What makes you good at...?'

'How do you do that?'

'What specifically do you do step by step?'

'What belief do you have at that point?'

Write the skills on their brick wall alongside their writing. They might be happy to write it themselves but I find I can write it in a way that clearly identifies the skill such that they can keep it as a reminder and show it to Mum and Dad as a tangible result of their session.

Do you notice that we are using the same sort of questions as we use for modelling? Why is that? It's because we are modelling their own excellence.

It is important to realise that skills have a sneaky habit of getting stuck in one place in our life and staying there, refusing to come out and refusing to be available when we need them elsewhere. The way we can tease them out of hiding is to tell them that we can see them. Perhaps you remember how as a child you'd put your hands over your face to 'hide' from your mum. Then you'd take your hands away and say 'Here I am,' but your mum could see you all the time, couldn't she? What we need to do is gently take those hands away and say 'I can see you' to those skills of ours and our clients. Be curious. I cannot stress enough that this is the most important quality you need in order to help children find their potential.

Now your client has a great sense of their own set of skills and you'll see them almost grow before your eyes. Ask them:

'Which of these skills will get you through that wall so you can achieve your compelling outcome?'

We are pretty much done now, but the final stage is to do an 'ecology' check:

f) Who else will it affect and what will that mean for you?

Children are not self-sufficient; other people need to do things for them. At school and at home there are those who have other people to consider so a child's needs cannot always be met. It is important for you and your client to check what their outcome will mean for them at home with their family and at school. Discuss how any resistance might be overcome.

Children sometimes say to me, "Can you ask Mum and Dad?"

The answer is a resounding, 'No!'

Why?

Because, of course, children have all the resources they need, and it could be that your next session might involve learning how to communicate in rapport. It is really important that children can step out of the role of 'victim' in the Drama Triangle and express their own needs rather than being helpless and powerless.

Have you had it before? If so, what happened?

The final check is whether this is an outcome with history. Has the child been in this situation before? What happened? Is there something different this time and if so, what?

Integration

I like to finish this off with a Circle of Excellence – one of my favourites. It is a great way to integrate the learning and fully embody the skills we've identified.

Exercise
You both need to stand up.
    '*What we're going to do now is called the* **Circle of Excellence**. *I want you to imagine that in front of you is a circle on the floor.*
    '*Imagine that all the skills you have identified are inside that circle. When I say "1,2,3, go!" step into the circle and bend down, pulling the circle up like a bubble with you inside – this is the 'skill bubble.' Then close your eyes and imagine having all those skills and getting that outcome.*
    Give the images and sounds and action, colour and clarity as if you were watching yourself doing it on the cinema screen. Give yourself a few minutes and as the image or feeling is fading, step back out of it.
    Break state – shimmy and a shake!
    Now this time when you step back in, imagine turning up the volume, the feeling, and the brightness when you've pulled up the skill bubble.
    Break state – shimmy and a shake.
    The last time, do it again and this time, push the bubble of skills out into your energy field and enjoy a sense of presence as you experience yourself with all these skills around you.
    Now put your thumb and index finger together to make a circle and bend down as if to scoop up your Circle of Excellence. Now put it in your pocket. This is your portable circle of excellence and you can use it whenever you want some confidence and access to those amazing skills and achieve your compelling outcome.
    Now 'Future Pace' it by asking your client to imagine using this to achieve their outcome next week or whenever they've said they would do this thing they've worked on.

Do you see how whatever you work on from their wish list will provide a whole heap of skills that can be integrated and anchored using the Circle of Excellence and be used for endless situations, any of which may also be on Mum and Dad's wish list?

Your client will leave feeling really resourced and know they've done the work themselves, which will ensure it is integrated much more than someone simply telling them what they're good at.

Another great NLP technique for working with compelling outcomes is Logical Levels of Change.

Exercise

Purpose –
Why am I
here?

Identity – Who
am I?

Beliefs & Values – What
matters to me?

Capabilities – What skills do I
have?

Behaviour – What do I do?

Environment – Where am I?

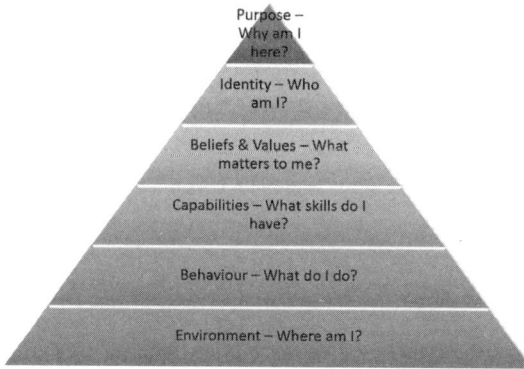

We start at the top and talk about what the child wants. This could be settling in happily at their new school, making new friends, doing well in some exams, 'improving their personal best in running. We write this down on the right-hand side of the chart alongside Purpose.

Now let's look at identity. This is about what sort of person they are, how they would describe themselves in the context of the goal they have set. For example, a good identity for someone who wants to improve their personal best in running would be 'an athlete'.

What beliefs and values do they have that support their purpose? How important is it to them and why is that? What is the bigger picture?

What skills do they have that will help them achieve this?

What do they currently do towards this goal?

Where do they do this?

Now we move to the other side of the chart, to the left-hand side and look at how the child or teen could align themselves even better towards achieving their purpose.

Where else could they do what they do? What other options are there?

What more could they do to achieve it?

What other skills could they learn that would help?

What other beliefs and values that they have in other areas of their life would help here?

Look again at identity, what else does that mean that they are?

In this exercise we are trying to align the child fully with what they want to achieve, their compelling outcome and looking for ways to build a really compelling picture and 'fill in the gaps' where they need to do more work or think differently.

Throughout the Logical Levels Technique we focus on what the child wants and the positive ways they can use their skills, qualities and experience to achieve it.

(3)

PERCEPTION OR FACT – OVERCOMING LIMITING BELIEFS

NLP, like a lot of modalities, talks a lot about beliefs, yet this is a word that isn't in common parlance. Most people talk about beliefs in relation to religion, don't they? Changing beliefs in that context might even be considered undesirable. When we talk about beliefs we are referring to what we hold to be true in the moment about our current situation. It is our internal representation of what has happened, what was said or done. It is based on our childhood, parents, schooling, experiences of life and the key events that have affected us, particularly those in the first six years of life.

Many of these beliefs will be helpful, such as: some snakes may be poisonous so we should be careful, or, it is important to look both ways before crossing a road. These beliefs keep us safe. However, we may also hold beliefs that don't keep us safe but instead hold us back from achieving all our capabilities. We call the beliefs that help us 'resourceful beliefs' because they give us the resources to move forward. The beliefs that don't help us we call 'limiting beliefs' because they limit what we can achieve or be in life.

What we want children to do is learn how to

o Notice a thought.
o Identify it as fact or belief.
o Is it helpful? If yes, act on it.
o Is it unhelpful? Apply one of the methods outlined in this chapter to overcome it.

There's a lovely exercise I do with children that I'd like to share with you. It's a fun way to help them recognise the difference between limiting and resourceful beliefs.

Exercise

Make a list of phrases that your child might say. Here's my list, designed to cover a range of children's ages. The more extreme these phrases are the better, and it's also essential that they reflect what a child might say. The child needs to recognise them as being something they might have said.

Girls can't catch a ball.
Boys are silly.
Homework is boring.
Vegetables are disgusting.
Football is the best sport ever.
History is easy.
Geography is interesting.
It's difficult to get to sleep.
Maths is hard.
The dark is scary.
My teacher is right.
English is boring.
Science is fun.
Trying new things is scary.
I can't get to sleep unless Mummy stays with me.
Making new friends is hard.
My teacher doesn't like me.
...and so on.

Then write some facts:

B comes after A in the alphabet.
We should look both ways before crossing a road.

Apples grow on trees.
Fruit is good for us.
We sleep in a bed.
The earth is round
Our Prime Minister is (correct name).
...and so on.

If you're a teacher or coach you may want to laminate the sheet and cut out the phrases so you have them in strips if you plan to use them a few times. Mix the strips up and ask your child to sort them into three groups:

a) Facts
b) Limiting beliefs – beliefs that don't help
c) Resourceful beliefs – beliefs that do help

Now go through each group. Check that the facts really are facts. Discuss what has to be true for something to be a fact. I usually say, 'A fact is something that everyone would agree is true with no exceptions.'

Question those phrases that they have said are facts but which you know are not. It's not unusual for children to say that 'homework is boring' is a fact and that everyone would agree that it is.

I ask, 'Can you think of even one person who would disagree?' If they can, then it can't be a fact.

Now take their limiting beliefs and ask them in what way each belief limits them or limits someone who believes that thing.

Perhaps they can give you an example of a limiting belief that has been an issue for them and you can discuss if that has always been the case. What has changed? If it has changed before, perhaps it can change again. It's useful for them to be curious about how they could open themselves up to the possibility that this belief is not a stuck state but simply a temporary state that they can overcome. How could they change the wording to enable them to move this to the group of resourceful beliefs? Sometimes just by adding the word 'yet', this can be possible. I know lots of teachers suggest this.

Discuss how they have overcome limiting beliefs in the past. Are there things they can do now that they struggled with? How did they overcome this struggle? What worked, what didn't work? In many ways NLP is about structure. Bandler and Grinder paid attention, in great detail, to what worked, how it worked and the underlying belief behind the excellence. I would really encourage you as coaches, parents, teachers, to use this fun exercise to lead onto a more in-depth discussion along these lines:

Can you think of something you used to find difficult but now find easy?

o *What changed?*
o *What did you do?*
o *What was the difference that made the difference?*
o *What change took place in the belief you had about this thing?*
o *How could you use that belief for things you feel you can't do now?*
o *Let's have a go.*

The resourceful beliefs may once have been limiting beliefs, and this will help them see how beliefs change with age, with knowledge, with experience and by perseverance, by stepping out of their comfort zone and finding out just how amazing they are. It's good for them to realise that beliefs, unlike facts, change.

Children experience limiting beliefs in different ways. To some extent, it may depend on whether the child is visual, auditory or kinaesthetic. A visual child might see the climbing wall as higher or see a new situation as scarier. An auditory child might hear a voice as more shouty or harsher and a kinaesthetic child may feel an atmosphere as more dangerous.

I know that before I learnt about NLP I would dismiss my children's limiting beliefs. Their 'I can't' would be met with 'of course you can' or 'you can do this'. Of course, this doesn't really help, because not only was I not being helpful but I was suggesting they were wrong.

A more helpful response, I know now, is to accept that this is how they feel right now and trust that they can overcome the block by looking at the choices they have. Here's an example relating to homework which I know a lot of children struggle with and parents aren't sure how to help them with.

o   Re-read the question
o   Take a break from it for a few minutes
o   Have some water
o   Have a snack
o   Get some fresh air
o   Think about how great you'll feel when you've done it

Remember, *if you always do what you've always done, you will always get what you've always got.* So, do something different and encourage them to do something different too. I have spoken to many parents who say that their children say they can't do their homework every day and eventually, after much stress and coaxing, it gets done but it still happens regularly.

Another idea to bear in mind is that there's a positive intention behind every behaviour and children may be enjoying the attention they're getting for their 'I can't' even if it is negative attention.

Some children experience limiting beliefs like a wall blocking their path, or it could be a little voice in their head telling them they can't do something, or a sick feeling in their stomach. How they express it is the phrase 'I can't...' sometimes accompanied by a victim type of pose with head down, shoulders hunched and lack of eye contact, fidgeting and mumbling.

I remember my grandpa used to say, 'Come on, laddy, look up, shoulders back and off we go'. The mere act of looking up and pushing our shoulders back, tells our body we are OK and it gives the brain a positive message. The fastest way to change our state is by changing our physiology. Moving really helps.

It is interesting how eye accessing can alter perceptions. In some way, our eyes can alter how we feel about something depending on where we look.

Here's an experiment to try quickly now:

Think of something you can't do...
Now look up and picture yourself struggling to do this thing.
Now look up to the right and imagine yourself doing it. (or the left if you are left handed).
Now say, 'What if I could do this thing?'

What you're doing is acting 'as if' and changing your physiology as you do it. Looking up to the left is where your visual memories are held and looking directly up is connecting to the present. Looking up to the right is where you construct new visual memories.

We all have limiting beliefs and many of us can avoid thinking about them by simply not doing them. I know a lot of people who would avoid doing a Facebook Live or a Webinar, leading a workshop or phoning a potential client.

But we can't simply avoid doing anything difficult. Not only does this encourage our children to do the same but also you might simply have to one day. For example, you might suddenly find yourself in a situation where, despite being scared of heights, you find you have to face a steep set of stairs down a fire escape because the lift is out of action.

Children have very little control of their environment so they really need strategies for managing and overcoming limiting beliefs because things will happen in their life that they have to cope with.

Here are the steps to overcoming limiting beliefs:

1) The first thing to do when you encounter a Limiting Belief is to accept it.

Acknowledging your feelings, and allowing your child or client to accept their feelings, calms down the anxiety and stops the fight/flight response by breathing into that feeling and giving it some love. Putting in a pause into our behaviour or thought allows us to decide how to tackle the feelings, and there are a number of ways to do this which I will take you through.

2) The next stage is to be curious.

'Where did that come from?' you might ask yourself. Accept it as a curiosity. There's no point rejecting it or arguing with it until you know something about it. This is what you're going to be working with.

o Where did this belief come from?
o Is it yours or is it inherited from mum or dad?
o Who told you it was true?
o What if it wasn't true and is just a belief not a fact?
o Is it always true in every situation that you can't do this thing?
o When can you do this thing, how did you do it on that occasion?
o Have you done something similar?
o Is it still true today that you can't do this thing?

Limiting beliefs come from childhood and from one's upbringing. Sometimes they are directly inherited from parents, so you will have a child who believes they are shy and daren't speak up because their mother is also shy and has unwittingly passed on the behaviour and the belief that this is what 'we' do. I had a client this week who has trouble sleeping and this went back to her grandma whose husband worked in a dangerous role at night during the war and she had young babies. It's remarkable to think that while her grandma was keeping herself awake at night this pattern was picked up by her mum, and now her.

They can stem from being told repeatedly that the child is stupid, no good at Maths, naughty, etc. and children take on this limiting belief as part of their identity because they've been told it by someone they respect, or by a parent or teacher, etc.

TIME LINE WITH ANCHORING

The Time Line is a fantastic technique for working with limiting beliefs because it introduces children and teens to the idea that they may not always have had this belief and they may not have it in the future. It shows them a world of possibilities as opposed to the stuck state they may be feeling in right now.

Start by introducing your child to their Time Line by asking them to imagine a line along the floor going from birth to when they are really old (around 20yrs of age!) and ask them to stand on the point representing today.

Be aware that some people want the line going through them front to back and others have it through them horizontally. Some walk sideways along it and others turn and face the way they're going. It really doesn't matter so long as wherever they are on the Time Line they are associated fully into it. It is their Time Line and they have full control over it. Whatever is happening on their Time Line when they guess, they access their subconscious mind, which is where they have that intuitive 'knowing'. They are also fully present wherever they are on the Time Line so we use the present tense asking, 'Where are you now?' or 'What is happening at this stage in your life?'

Exercise

They start at the present on the Time Line and talk about how they feel, what they'd like to be able to do, their compelling outcome in effect. Then they talk about what's stopping them, their Limiting Belief.

We aren't born with Limiting Beliefs, we acquire them so even if children say they have 'never' been able to do this thing or that they 'always' thought this way, it simply isn't true, although of course it is true for them at a conscious level.

Ask them to go back to a time in the past when they were able to do that thing.

If they can't think of a time, and with younger children that might well be the case, ask them to go to a future time when they will be able to do it, believe it or feel it.

At that point, be it past or future, we do an anchoring process. Here's how it goes:

Step 1. Association into the belief

'Tell me about having this belief that you can (say the resourceful belief) what's it like to believe that you can (resourceful belief)

- o *What can you do?*
- o *What else can you do?*
- o *What's the feeling?*
- o *Is there a sound, what can you hear when you can...?*
- o *What can you see?*
- o *What can you smell?*
- o *What can you taste?*

When you feel totally connected and aligned with this belief, put your hands together, do a 'thumbs up' or you can choose whatever action you like for this process and you might like to agree what it will be before doing the process with your client.

As you notice them disconnecting a bit, maybe they open their eyes or you see them relax a bit, ask them to 'break state'. This means to do a little jiggle or move their body to break the state. You then repeat the same anchoring process twice more.

Then to remind them, say that they can use this anchor whenever they want, to remind them of this belief.

With children, I may use metaphors and animals work really well.

'What animal or bird are you when you have this belief?' and you can decide on an action that reminds them of the animal and use that as their anchor.

Step 2. Walk back to the present spot using the anchor.

'Thinking again about that thing you want to do. How do you feel now?'
    Then ask them to go to a place on the Time Line in the future when they will do the thing they want to do. Using their anchor, how do they feel about doing this?
    Having anchored their resourceful belief, you'll find they feel much more positive now. There could be more work to do, though, and often this will be around psychological reversal and the positive benefits of keeping at least some resistance.
    Good questions to ask are:
    o What does having this limiting belief enable you to do?
    o What does having this limiting belief get you out of doing?

The Time Line is a great tool for challenging perceptions and beliefs because it offers clients the possibility to imagine life without them, in the past and in the future.

PERCEPTUAL POSITIONING

This is another great tool to use for limiting beliefs. Using three chairs or cushions we can create three 'positions'.

Position 1 is 'I'. 'I' is me. It represents what the client wants, their compelling outcome, what they want to do.

Position 2 is the limiting belief 'You'. This is the thing that is stopping them and it's sitting in the chair opposite them.

For clarity and fun, I often use glove puppets or cuddly toys so they can clearly know that these are different positions. It's like the two parts of your mind; the one part that wants something and the other part that is saying, 'You can't do this'.

Position 3 is the impartial bystander, like a closed-circuit camera. It has no emotions regarding these two parts and has no investment in the exchange. It is there to observe and compute, nothing more.

Exercise

I explain the three positions and ask the client which chair they'd like for themselves as the 'I' position. They can then place themselves on it together with the cuddly toy or puppet they have chosen. Obviously, this isn't necessary but I like to inject some fun into my sessions. Essentially, I want them to enjoy getting to know themselves and how their mind works.

They then choose which chair is for the Limiting Belief and put another cuddly toy in it.

The last chair is obviously then the 'other' or third position and doesn't need a toy because it's like a computer.

Step 1.

Sitting in Position 1, the child tells Position 2 what they want to do.
'I want to...'
When they've said this, I ask them to stand up, put the cuddly toy on that seat and break state.
Break state is when they have a jiggle, or a little wiggle and move their body to indicate a change from position 1 to Position 2.
They then move to Position 2 and pick up the other cuddly toy and speak as their Limiting Belief. They express whatever it is that is holding position 1 back. For example:
'You can't do that, you aren't brave enough.'
'You'll make an idiot of yourself.'
'You'll look stupid.'
'You'll fail and then you'll feel bad.'
Again, once they've spoken they stand up, put the bear or toy on the seat and break state before returning to Position 1 to respond.
The conversation continues between the two parts or positions as they get closer to Position 1 being able to convince Position 2 that they can manage whatever Position 2 is putting in their way.
As the facilitator, I make sure that Position 1 understands that Position 2 has a positive intention. Position 2 is part of them and in some

way wants to look after them, keep them safe and doesn't want them to feel bad, fail or get hurt physically, mentally or emotionally.

Understanding the positive intention is important in this exercise and often I find that once the client has understood this positive intention and worked out how they can reassure it that they are not needed and that they can cope with whatever fallout there may be as a result of them doing the thing they want to do, the exercise finishes fairly soon after.

Once there seems to be resolution, they move to position 3 where they sit and reflect on what they've heard from Position 1 and Position 2, and sum up what the resolution is that they have come to.

What we want to achieve is for your child client to recognise that their limiting belief:

o   Is not their fault
o   They can change it to a resourceful belief
o   Has a positive intention
o   Can still have the positive intention but use a resourceful belief in its place
o   Is theirs, and it is their choice to keep it or get rid of it

This is a great exercise to do as the client gets the chance to associate into each position and understand the different parts of themselves that come into play when they have a Limiting Belief.

PARTS INTEGRATION

In this technique, we are examining those situations in which we feel torn in two directions. This could involve a limiting belief or a conflict with someone. I've used it for sibling rivalry, conflict with a parent or teacher or friend. In every case there is already a limiting belief to explore and clear.

This exercise has the same concept as Perceptual Positioning but doesn't require chairs or cushions. It works better online and it is one that I teach children to use when they have an obstacle or block while at school.

Exercise

I ask them to hold out both hands face upwards. They must choose one hand in which to hold the compelling outcome and the other holds their Limiting Belief or person with whom there is conflict.

Step 1.

Ask, 'Which hand feels heavier?'

Start with the heavier hand. For this example, we will start with the Limiting Belief.

'Looking at the hand holding the Limiting Belief. What do you see? If there was an animal or bird there, what would it be? Tell me about it. Is there an object there? Is there a colour?'

Explore with them everything about what's in that hand.

We are asking them to associate into it.

'I'd like to ask it what it wants for you.'

They will then tell you.

Now go to the hand holding the compelling outcome. Ask:

'Looking at the hand holding the Compelling Outcome. What do you see? If there was an animal or bird there, what would it be? Tell me about it. Is there an object there? Is there a colour?'

Explore with them everything to do with what's in that hand.

We are asking them to associate into it.

'I'd like to ask it what it wants for you.'

They will then tell you.

'Now, close your eyes and imagine the conversation between them as each argues their point. Remember to listen out for the positive intention of each hand. They are both parts of you. They both want what's best for you. How can you reassure the hand holding the Limiting Belief that you can manage whatever it fears for you?'

Once the conflict has been resolved, ask them to bring both hands to their heart and I usually invite them to flood their heart with a colour that represents resolution, whatever that colour may be for them.

POSTCARD TO A LIMITING BELIEF

This is a great exercise to finish off any work you've done on Limiting Beliefs.

Exercise

Ask them to write a postcard to their limiting belief.

'Imagine that this belief of yours has gone away on holiday and you want to write them a postcard to tell them to stay away. Tell them how much happier you are without them and what you are able to do without them around.'

In these times of Covid-19 when I'm writing, I have changed this to:

'Imagine that this belief of yours is stuck in another country and can't get back because they are in lockdown. You want to write to them to tell them to stay there and take a holiday. Tell them how much happier you are without them and what you are able to do without them around.'

This is a writing exercise so if you have a younger child or one who doesn't fancy writing then use an object (I might use a glove puppet) and imagine that this is their limiting belief.

'What would you like to say or do to this limiting belief?'

I'm often asked about terminology: whether I use the NLP terminology or make up other words. I always use the NLP terminology because I feel it is respectful of children to do so. There is nothing difficult about the words 'limiting belief' or 'resourceful belief' and I would explain by saying a resourceful belief is a belief that helps you and a limiting belief is one that stops you, or limits you.

(4)

CLEARING NEGATIVE THOUGHTS AND FEELINGS USING EFT TAPPING

The Emotional Freedom Technique is a meridian energy technique which involves tapping on specific acupuncture points as we say words reminding us of the issue or challenge we face. It is usually known as 'Tapping'.

EFT developed out of TFT (Thought Field Therapy) which was discovered by Dr Roger Callahan in the 1980s when he was using the Chinese meridian points with his patients, tapping on the meridian point that connected to their pain or illness. One of his students, Gary Craig, further developed it by reducing the tapping points and creating a simple sequence which became known as the Emotional Freedom Technique in 1990. So, whilst it is based on ancient Chinese medicine, the protocol is relatively new compared to NLP.

Whilst NLP might be described as a talking therapy, EFT is an energy healing modality, which means that there is very little talking, and it is what we call clean language because we use a series of questions to set up the process and then just tap on the points and say the client's words.

Later in this chapter I will also describe PTT (Picture Tapping Technique) which adds in drawing to the mix of tapping and clean language.

I discovered EFT at a local ANLP (Association of Neuro-Linguistic Programming) Practice Group. I run our local group and we regularly have demos to keep us all on our toes. On this occasion, Chrys Fisher did an EFT demo, and I was so moved by how effective it was. I then embarked on what has become ongoing training. It sparked such interest in Energy Healing and how we can connect energetically with our clients and minimise words, story and clutter. By 'clutter' I mean the numerous ways in which we attract the stories we created in our first six years of life, and even sometimes at birth.

The great thing about working with children and teens and being a parent, or teacher, or indeed any coach of young people, is that we can catch these stories and guide our clients through the process of changing them so they can have the rest of their life to reap the benefits. It always feels a bit sad to me when I treat an older person with, say, 'shame' or the feeling that 'I'm not loved' or 'I'm not worthy of love', 'I'm not good enough', noting how they have by then had a lifetime of attracting these stories, experiencing unhealthy relationships and not fulfilled their potential. It's great to see that burden removed with such an enormous sense of relief. Since becoming an EFT practitioner and trainer I have attracted many more non-child clients, especially mums, wanting to clear their blocks so they can be a better parent.

NLP does a fabulous job and the philosophy and techniques are a strong core to have in any modality, be it hypnotherapy, reflexology, counselling, and all the others.

What I love about EFT, though, is the lack of story, the lack of content and how it goes straight to the pain, the grief, anger, sadness without the back story. These techniques enable us to work content-free (story-free). There are a number of reasons why we might want to do this.

CLIENTS WHO ARE TOTALLY INTO THEIR HEAD.

All the chatter, the story, the 'who did what, when' and the history of the issue are at the forefront, and so when they come in and sit down, they say, 'Gosh, I don't know where to start.' My first thought is to start where they are right now. Start with the feeling about all of this story. 'When you think of all this thing that you want me to know, what is the feeling? Where is it in your body, what's the colour?' and we get tapping.

You can do this with your children, too. When they come back from school saying 'he did this' or 'she did that', ask them to just tune into the feeling and get tapping to clear it.

Talking can just take us round and round in circles. This approach gets them into their subconscious, the emotions, and into their body. This is truer for adults, and when I am working with parents, particularly mums, to help them with their relationship with their children, it always goes back to their childhood. This means there is a lot of story and the bit I need is buried in their subconscious mind. It will be about what they made something mean when they were too young to understand the story. The shock at the time sent them into 'freeze' and they formed that core belief that they then live out, attracting evidence of its truth throughout their life. Rather than hearing all these examples, it is much more efficient and respectful of their time, I feel, to get straight into the feeling and tap on those negative feelings to clear them.

Example

Yesterday I had a client who felt she wasn't good enough. Whenever she didn't understand what someone was saying or couldn't work out how to do something when things went wrong, or when her children played up, her core belief kicked in, which was, 'I'm not good enough', and she felt sad and alone.

When we started tapping on this feeling 'dark sludgy feeling in my tummy' I asked her how old she was when she had this dark sludgy feeling in her tummy'. Because she has no confidence about her ability to be right she said, 'I don't know.'

'...and if you did know...? I asked. 'Just guess.'

'Four,' she said.

'And what had just happened when you had this dark sludgy feeling in your tummy and you're four?'

'The teacher told me that what I did wasn't very good.'

'What did you make that mean?' I asked.

'That I'm stupid, I don't know anything, I'm wrong.'

'And what decision did you make in that moment?'

'That no one will listen to me, that I get things wrong.'

So, not too surprising then when you have a belief like this that you would perhaps express yourself in a way that shows you expect not to be listened to.

'Every day I tell Benny to brush his teeth and he doesn't listen to me.'

We used the Time Line, a classic NLP technique to go back to her four-year-old self and had a little chat with her younger self and (in her imagination) invited in another teacher who was much kinder. My client connected to her younger self and with the teacher, and had an imaginary conversation where the other teacher told her that sometimes people say unkind, thoughtless things, and that she must believe in herself. My client also said to me that perhaps this had to happen for her to understand that getting things wrong is part of the learning process.

Example

I was doing an editing job when I was last in Australia; it was a children's book. I was having a cup of tea with the author and just chatting about my work and telling her that I work on negative beliefs. She told me that she'd like some help. Her book was due to be published and she knew she'd get a big advance. Her worry was that she would spend it.

'I just can't keep hold of money,' she said. 'I'm worried I'll spend it all.'

We tapped on the feeling of 'not being able to keep hold of money' and where it was in the body – the colour, shape, emotions (shame, disappointment, embarrassment, sadness) and the intensity of the feeling (the SUDs level – this is the Subjective Units of Distress scale, with zero being 'no stress' and ten being 'maximum stress') came down but there was still some feeling of shame. I asked her:

'How old are you when you have that feeling of shame in your solar plexus (many clients are familiar with the chakras and refer to them in their tapping)?'

'I'm five and we're at the pier. Mummy has just given each of us girls a $5 note to spend on the games. I was waving it about and it flew out of my hand. I went to Mummy and she was very cross. She said, 'You just can't keep hold of anything.''

It would be great to say that we can get rid of negative core beliefs as profound as this in one session of tapping and work on our younger self (Matrix Reimprinting). We can when we work with children, as their belief was imprinted quite recently, but for adults it will take more sessions, more time, and many more visits to those early memories and the various different aspects of them.

Mums and Dads and teachers are people of influence. What we say matters. Sadly, and completely unintentionally, we say something in a moment of anger which may be completely unrelated to our child but because of the influence we have, they create in that moment a UDIN.

A UDIN is:

Unexpected
Dramatic
Isolating
No strategy

So, my client, the author, had this precious gift of $5 and unexpectedly it flew out of her hand. Her mum's reaction was dramatic. In that moment she felt isolated. Although her mum was physically there, she was unavailable. She had no strategy to resolve her situation. She froze, and in that moment of freeze, she imprinted the belief that money flies out of her hand; she can't hold onto it. Can you see how easy it is for a seemingly insignificant event to create a lifetime of attracting evidence of its truth? It becomes our story. My client wasn't spending money on herself. She was spending it on the home, on her family and children in particular, as well as on her friends and her own parents. But she wasn't saving it, so she always felt she needed to be earning more, and this created its own stress. She was constantly telling herself she needed more work, I won't say what she does as this would identify her, but there was a lot of chatter justifying her overworking. Underpinning the chatter was this core belief about money flying out of her hand. Tapping on her younger self allowed her to create a different belief.

When clients come into my therapy room chatting non-stop, I suggest a few deep breaths and a round of tapping to see where we go with it, just to clear what they come in with. This may or may not be the issue they want to work on but it is probably related to it in some way. It is our job as therapists and parents to find linking patterns of beliefs and to be curious about how these beliefs may be preventing clients from achieving our higher purpose.

WHEN CLIENTS ARE IN EMOTIONAL OVERWHELM.

Some clients just don't know what they feel any more. There are so many emotions and they can't see a way forward. They will be tearful and tired, feeling like they can barely function. By using this approach, we give them a tool they can use to manage the emotions as they come up.

I'd love to say I can offer clients appointments the same day as they contact me but that isn't possible. They will, therefore, by the time they arrive, have been thinking about what they want to work on with me, thinking about what's on their mind and they make sure they use the time productively. Child clients may have been worrying about what I will ask (they will already have met me with their parent at the 90-minute introductory session) and also they will have been more focused on their problem knowing they will be seeing me. It's my job to put them at their ease with some fun activities designed to understand what's going on for them, but tapping can be a great way to reduce initial anxiety and settle them down.

Overwhelm happens more often with parents who come to a session planning to address one issue and then find loads of other issues tumbling into the story – from their childhood, perhaps their mum's childhood, or relationship issues they hadn't planned to bring up. This overwhelm can cause them to sob and feel uncomfortable. Tapping can be comforting as they breathe and tap on all the things that are emerging once the metaphorical tap starts to flow.

WHEN YOU NEED TO WORK CONTENT-FREE

EFT really comes into its own in this instance. This might be because your child or client doesn't want to tell you the story itself. Perhaps they worry that you, the parent or teacher, will take it up with the school or their friend's parent and they just want comfort and their distress eased without having to tell you what's happened. I also find that adult clients, mums and dads in my practice, may feel ashamed of something they've said or done and want to make sure it doesn't happen again rather than have to relive the incident. I've certainly worked with lots of teenagers and young people who would prefer that their parents didn't know what was happening, so...

Example

It was an introductory session for a boy aged 12 and his mum was present as is nearly always the case for first appointments. As the child was talking about his anxiety, his mum was clearly struggling to hold back her emotion. I suggested to the boy I do something to help his mum but I didn't want her to have to share what she was upset about with her son in case it wasn't appropriate. So, I explained the tapping concept and we quickly went to the breathing to calm her down. We then did the set up like this:

'Even though I'm upset right now, I totally love and accept myself anyway,' three times as usual.

Then we tapped round the body with her son tapping along for the borrowed benefits:

'Feeling upset.'

'Upset.'

I then asked where it was in her body and the colour and we added that in.

'Yellow upset in my tummy.'

It soon eased and changed to 'embarrassment' and then disappeared. I then resumed working with her son who was mighty impressed by the tapping.

Exercise

If you are a teacher or a coach working with a group in a workshop or classroom situation, it is much more effective to work content-free because they may not want to share what's on their mind.

Ask the class to tune in to whatever is on their mind, whatever might be worrying or annoying them. You can do this online as well. Ask them to close their eyes, put their hands to their heart and reflect on what's not OK right now. If you are working online they can turn their videos off and mute themselves if they want.

Then start the tapping off with the usual set-up:

'Even though I'm not feeling great right now, I love and accept myself anyway.'

Or:

'Even though I have sad feelings, I love and accept myself anyway.'

Or:

'Even though I feel annoyed right now, I love and accept myself anyway.'

Remember, you the teacher or workshop leader will also be benefiting from this as you all tap together so this will calm everyone down. If you have classroom assistants in the room, they can tap as well.

Then you do two rounds of tapping through the usual points that are described below.

Either they can tap on their own specific feelings silently or 'on mute,' or you can choose a global phrase to lead them in the tapping, such as:

'All these feelings.'

Although they will all be saying the same thing, the words will connect to their own individual feelings so will still be relevant to each person, albeit differently.

We can tap on:

'that thing that happened.'
'what I did.'

'what I said.'

'the thing I'm worried about.'

With PTT (picture tapping) that I'm going to describe shortly, you are simply tapping on the title of their picture or elements within it, so it is even more content free. STT (silent tapping) is completely content-free.

If there is someone else in the room and you're wanting to help your child or client knowing they wouldn't want to share the story, again you can tap on 'what's just happened'.

I would normally do the full exploration of the feelings, colour and location at the beginning but I wanted to move quickly into the tapping so she could feel calmer as she seemed to be embarrassed, crying in front of him.

Schools where they have used tapping in the classroom, every morning at registration and after lunch break, have reported increased concentration in the lesson because children are not upset or anxious. They have also noticed increased compassion and understanding between children in the playground as they have a tool they can use, a universal language for helping someone with whatever they are struggling with.

Now I've told you all the many many ways we use EFT, here's how to do it.

THE EFT PROCESS

First explain to your client or your child what we're doing. This is what I say:

'Sometimes we work on issues and sometimes we work on feelings that relate to the issues. Our feelings live in our body. We then send the message up to the brain to try and work out what that feeling is or what it means but this doesn't always help. The brain sends the message back saying 'I've no idea what's going on here'. The body then experiences confusion, worry, feels unsafe and anxious and sends that message to the brain and so it goes on. What we're doing when we tap is working directly with the feeling as it moves around the body.

The language of your subconscious mind is images and colour, so we'll be exploring our feelings in that way.

The Emotional Freedom Technique or EFT is an energy healing modality. The body is made up of energy and water. Positive energy is light and allows us to flow and feel aligned and connected with our higher self. Negative energy is lumpy and blocks that flow making us feel sad and lethargic and stuck.'

I make sure there's plenty of water to hand and a box of tissues because when we shift energy and clear emotions in our body we often cry. They can be tears of relief that we have freed ourselves from these heavy energies, tears of anger at having held onto them for so long, tears of grief at losing something that had become part of our identity, and tears of sadness for the years we've spent holding onto the pain. This doesn't usually happen with children, though. Children clear their emotions quickly and efficiently and very few cry. Teenagers may express more emotion as they've had longer with them. The most emotional are parents because they have the added sadness of potentially having passed their negative beliefs onto their children.

I pre-frame the session therefore by saying that they may feel weepy and that's fine, it's good, it's the energy moving and processing the emotions. I ask them to let me know when emotions change and when anything comes up that has shifted things. I feel that EFT is a beautiful collaborative process where I am holding the space for my client to do the work. I don't need to know everything that's going on, all their thoughts and feelings. I only need to tap along with them, repeating the words they give me, the colours, images, feelings.

The first thing we do in any EFT session is to tune in.

1. Tuning in

Drink some water. Breathe. Put your hand on your heart and close your eyes.

Breathe in for 6 and out for 6. Imagine you're breathing into your heart.

Do this three times.

Now, thinking about the situation or issue on your mind:

- What's the feeling or emotion?
- Where is it in the body?
- What colour is it?
- What shape, texture, size? (for size you can ask is it the size of a grape or a melon or...)
- Is it static or moving?
- Is there anything else about it?

SUDS level – on a scale of 0-10 where zero is nothing and 10 is very intense, what number would you give this feeling?

I make notes of all the above to ensure that I only use their words and don't misremember or paraphrase their words or correct them. It's tempting when children use the wrong word for an emotion, to correct it. For example, some may say 'anxiousness' and you correct it to 'anxiety'. What they call their feeling is what we tap on because it is essential that it connects directly to their emotions whatever they call them, so you may find yourself tapping on 'wobbly feeling', or 'jelly legs', 'vomit' and so on.

2. Set up

You lead this part of the process so it is important to pre-frame it with your client or child saying something like, 'I'm going to say what we are tapping on and you will repeat it after me but if at any time I say something that isn't what you feel, because perhaps the feeling, colour or place in the body has changed, just tell me and we'll change it.'

Refer to your notes and start by tapping on the karate chop point. This is the fleshy part of the hand at the side, between the base of your little finger and your wrist.

'Even though I feel this (name of emotion) in my (part of the body) I love and accept myself anyway.'

Do this three times. You don't need to repeat exactly the same words although they must certainly be your client's words; you can vary it a bit and if they have different colours or emotions in different parts of the body you can spread them out across the three phases. For example,

'Even though I feel yellow shame in my tummy...'
'Even though I feel a tightness in my chest...'
'Even though I feel brown guilt on my shoulders...'
Make sure you breathe.

3. Tapping

Go to the first tapping point on the crown of your head. At this point I usually check whether anything else has come up because simply by doing the setup, this can trigger other feelings and things can move quite fast especially with children.

So tapping with the flat of your hand, or three fingers, you use a reminder phrase and tap through the points saying;

This (colour) (emotion)
All this (emotion)
(colour) (emotion)

Tapping points
Crown
Side of eye
Other side of eye
Under eye
Under nose
Under mouth
Collar bone
Side

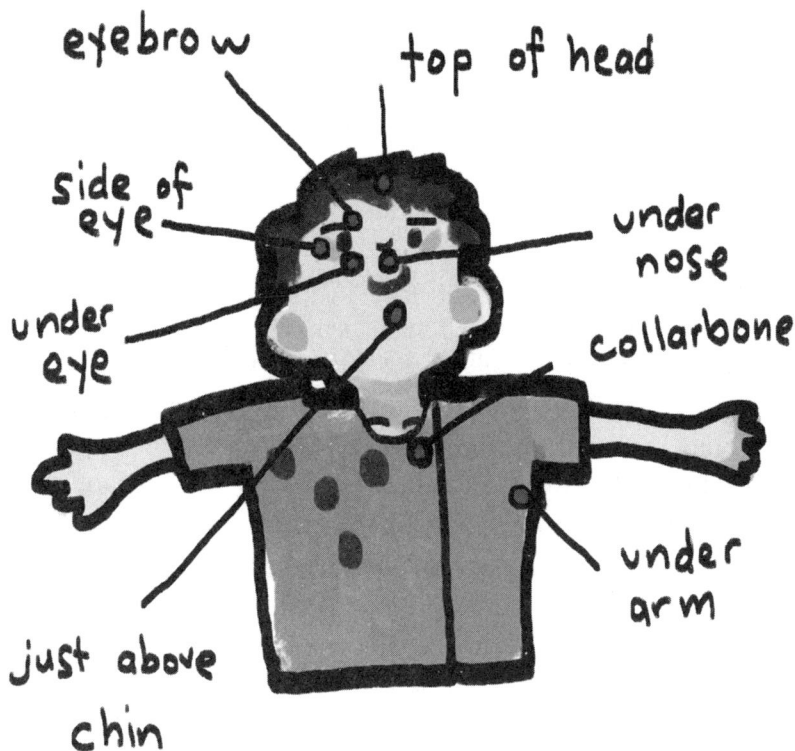

eyebrow
top of head
side of eye
under nose
under eye
collarbone
under arm
just above chin

I usually do two rounds of tapping through the body points and then move through the hand points because most of my clients are children and teens so they need to use these at school and around their friends as they can't suddenly start tapping their head.

Hand points are:
Across the wrist
Side of thumb
Side of index finger
Side of middle finger
Side of ring finger
Side of little finger

I go through these twice and then return to the karate chop point (side of hand) to check in with them as to what's happened.

I check:

SUDs level
Colours
Emotions
Locations

If the emotion has changed significantly from say 'feeling sad' to 'feeling angry', then I will repeat the set up using the new phrase and the whole set up process. If it has simply changed from, for example, 'I feel sad' to 'I feel lonely', I will check where the lonely feeling is, its colour and size and so on, then just continue tapping and changing the reminder phrases. Remember to only use their words. It's so important to maintain rapport in this process and keep the client in a meditative state so they don't go into their conscious mind trying to work out why.

4. Finishing

Once you are down to a SUDs level of zero you can, of course, stop, but I sometimes stop at a 1 or 2 if the client says they're feeling much better and that the feeling has gone. This is partly because children often want to keep a bit of anxiety in exam situations because they don't want to be so laid back they run out of time. Some want to leave it at 1 or 2 because that feels like enough of a shift to be getting along with right now, or they are just bored and want to do another activity.

If there was a situation or event or issue that had triggered the feelings, I ask them to think of that again so we can check whether we have cleared all the aspects. Every situation will have different 'scenes' or aspects and there is a specific technique I use called 'the movie' technique where we tap though each 'scene' stopping at every trigger and tapping to clear it before moving onto the next part of the story. If there are fresh aspects but you've run out of time, check that your client is OK for now and agree to work on the new aspect in your next session. With adults there are likely to be a number of aspects and many memories or events with triggers and beliefs. We may well want to go back in time, using the Time Line approach to find where the core belief was imprinted.

I know that this process keeps working after we have stopped tapping so although we may have stopped at 1 or 2, the chances are that it will drop below that, very quickly as the body moves the energy around.

I always go back through the process with them so they know what to do when they are on their own. Sometimes I send them a reminder video as well.

PTT – PICTURE TAPPING TECHNIQUE

PTT was developed by Phoenix EFT, although their work was predominantly with adults. I have developed it further using my own experience with children and through learning from other therapists and EFT Practitioners who work with children. This definition of the process is taken from the Phoenix EFT Training Manual.

'The main premise of PTT is that by asking the client to draw a sequence of pictures in a short space of time, we bypass the rational, thinking mind and this gives us access to the deeper, subconscious levels of the mind. The information accessed is drawn onto the paper as a series of coloured images which may or may not make any sense to the rational mind. Focusing just on the imagery produced rather than its meaning or emotional connotations allows easy and often emotion-free resolution of even complex issues.'

Interpretation of the pictures produced by a client is not required for the process to work and indeed is never done with the client unless they begin to make links and interpret for themselves. However, picture interpretation does greatly enhance the practitioner's understanding of the client's unique set of issues and can give useful insight about areas to explore in later sessions or with other methods.'

What I find beautiful about this method is that it is so 'clean'. It is cleaner than EFT in as much as the words we use are just the marks on their paper. We only repeat their words and let their subconscious mind make the connections as we tap alongside them and clear the emotions that they are struggling with. The client doesn't have to verbalise what they are feeling and the practitioner does not have to understand or interpret it. It is 'all about the process'. I find that my students are amazed at how effective this process is with no input from them at all apart from repeating the client's words, guiding the process and of course holding the space, which should not be underestimated.

This can be used by parents and teachers with whom children may be reluctant to share at a deep or intimate level because there could be repercussions if too much information is shared. Once they have cleared it, they may be more willing to share, once they feel less overwhelmed, confused or upset.

Just as with EFT, you need plenty of water and tissues. You will also need masses of white A4 plain paper and a good selection of felt pens – broad line multi-colour and black. Note that lots of sets of felt pens do not include black so you may need to buy them separately.

I also do a version of this with LEGO Serious Play. It's like LEGO but is designed for therapy, so instead of having hundreds of identical colour bricks, there is an assortment of all colours, numerous different bits and bobs that allows clients to be really creative and express themselves without words. As with the drawing, we tap on the bricks used, so:

green brick
three red bricks
window
curly tube

There are no figures in this set and that is important because we want clients to project onto the LEGO their own thoughts and feelings. So if you are creating your own set, remember to take out the figures and check you have all the colours represented because the language of the subconscious mind is colour and image.

You don't want your clients taking their models home so let them take a photo at the end if they want to reflect on the changes between each LEGO model. Apart from the fact that this is LEGO and the PTT standard process is drawing, the process itself is no different.

I use a sand tray with clients as you'll read about in the Art Therapy chapter and this too can be used in this technique. Be experimental. Use what you have; it's a great technique. Now I'll explain the details of how to do it.

EXPLANATION TO CLIENT

Our body is made up of energy and water. When we feel sad, anxious or angry these negative emotions block the energy pathways in our body and we feel stuck. Maybe we try to make sense of them in our head, but these emotions are actually in our body, and relate to our subconscious mind. Often they are triggers or reminders of feelings that go back to our early childhood, possibly before we even have memories.

What I'm going to ask you to do is to 'tune in' by putting your hands to your heart and closing your eyes. I'll ask you to breathe deeply into your heart and think about the thing that's bothering you. Imagine that it's happening right now. Then when you've done that, I want you to draw those feelings on the paper.

This won't be a picture like you'd put up on the wall, but just imagine those thoughts and feelings had colour, shape and so on. They can be squiggles, lines, circles etc. There will be between 5-7 pictures in this exercise and each time they will be slightly different.

In between each picture we will do something called EFT or tapping where we will tap on different meridians in the body – energetic pathways – and as we do that we will just say the colour and the emotion that it reminds you of. I won't ask you about the event or the situation but as you tap, your subconscious knows what you're tapping on, I don't need to know. We only tap on the negatives, though, so when you don't have any more negative emotions around the issue we're working on, let me know. OK, any questions?

1. Set Up

Drink some water.
 Tune in as for EFT.

Breathe into heart area for 6 and out, etc.

'Focus on the thing that's on your mind and when you're ready, if you were to draw a picture of how this issue makes you feel then what would you draw?'

Check if they want to add anything – is it complete?

'If it had a title can you write what it would be on the paper.'

It's not unusual for clients to say they don't know what the title would be and, in these situations, I suggest they close their eyes and put their hands on the picture and ask it, 'What would you like to be called?' If nothing comes up then simply use 'Don't know' as the title. Similarly, if they don't know what to draw we can tap on 'blank sheet of paper'. This is such a good technique for overwhelm, I've sometimes found big shifts after tapping on 'blank sheet of paper' or 'don't know'.

Now start the set up:

'Even though I've drawn this picture and I've called it (title) I love and accept myself anyway.'

Do this three times as for EFT. I sometimes change it each time. These are options I sometimes use:

'Even though I've drawn this picture and I've called it (title) that's OK for now and I love and accept myself anyway.'

'Even though I've drawn this picture and I've called it (title) it's a step in the process and I love and accept myself anyway.'

2. Two Tapping rounds

I remind them that we are just saying factually what they've drawn in the order they drew it. They need to simply say the colour and the description in the order they drew them. If you're doing this as an online session you won't know the order but face to face you can remind them. Go through the picture as you tap round the points.

Top of the head – '...and in this picture I have drawn...'

Example – Long green line/red circle, etc.

Then do a second round of tapping.

I add in more clean questions here.

'Tell me about the green, what is green?' (looking for the emotion – NOT the story)

Do the same for each colour and for line/circle/zig zag, coloured in, and so on. You may well see repeated colours across the pictures so you can check if the colour still means the same thing.

3. Continuing the process for next pictures

Continue the process by asking them to turn over the paper having written a 1 in the corner so if their pictures get muddled up, they know the order.

I ask them to have some water and tune in again. Then when they're ready ask, 'If you were to draw a picture of how this issue makes you feel now, what would you draw this time?'

Invite them to drink water, breathe, tune in and draw.

Repeat the steps exactly as before.

Notice colours and lines changing.

Check when you think you've got to resolution.

When you have resolution you don't tap.

4. Resolution

They draw their resolution picture in the same way as the other pictures, giving it a title but instead of tapping on it, ask, 'If you were to put a frame around this resolution picture, what colour or combination of colours would that frame be?'

Ask them to tune in again. These are the words to use now to imprint the resolution for your client.

'I want you to take this (colour) of the frame of your resolution picture and bring it into your head, down through your body, singing and dancing through every cell and fibre of your body, down through your legs and to the centre of the earth. Then bring that (colour) back up through your body into your heart space. Let that (colour) of your (title) of your resolution picture fill every part of your heart until it's bursting with that (colour) of (title) and when you're ready let it burst out and fill the energy field around you.'

Pause for them to integrate the resolution and the colour. Then say, 'When you're ready open your eyes and come back to the room.'

Check how they feel now.

You don't need to know what this was about but if they want to tell you that's fine. Don't comment, just listen.

They may want to look back through their pictures, that's fine of course.

9-STEP GAMUT

This can form a part of your process in EFT when the SUDs level seems to be a bit stuck, not reducing as you'd expect and I also teach it to children who struggle with concentrating or focus.

Use two fingers to tap the back of the hand in the space between the base of the little finger and the ring finger (the gamut point) then

- o Eyes up
- o Eyes down
- o Eyes left
- o Eyes right
- o Rotate eyes clockwise
- o Rotate eyes anti clockwise
- o Hum
- o Count to 9
- o Hum

I find that when you go back to the tapping again, the SUDs level has dropped quite a bit.

EFT can be used on phobias and fears, anxiety and stress, panic attacks, sleep problems, relationship issues, anger, pain, grief, lack of motivation and fear of performance.

PTT GROUP WORK

Like EFT, PTT can be used in a group or in class at school, workshops and so on. We need to pre-frame that

1) We will clear everyone's issues in 5 pictures.
2) We need to keep everyone at the same speed and reimprint at the same time, otherwise, as you can imagine, we are reimprinting one person's resolution picture while others are still clearing.
3) If someone resolves in fewer than 5 pictures they still have to wait for the others in the group but at least there is a finite end and the process won't be dragging on waiting for someone who is still resolving after 8 or 9.
4) To help manage the flow, we need to give everyone a time limit for their picture, say one minute. This has the benefit of preventing people going into conscious mind. We want them to access the subconscious mind.

Of course everyone needs paper, felt pens of a wide variety of colours, including black.

Explain that there will be a set number of pictures in the process.

'We are going to resolve this in 5 pictures because we have found that 5 pictures gives enough time to resolve issues without it being boring for those who resolve in fewer who then have to wait for the others to finish.

You will have one minute to draw each picture. When you feel that your issue is resolved just stop after you've written the title on it and use the 'raise your hand' to let me know. When everyone has a raised hand we will reimprint together. Any questions in the chat box?'

START THE PROCESS

Think of an issue to work on.

Give it a SUDS level.

'If you were to draw a picture of how this issue makes you feel, then what would that picture look like?'

Time 1 minute.

'If your picture had a title what would the title of that picture be? Please write the title on the picture.'

'Even though I've drawn this picture and I've called it... I love and accept myself anyway.'

Do this three times.

'And in this picture I have drawn...'

Two rounds of tapping (just body) as you look at your picture and tap on red line, blue circle, green square, black wiggles, etc.

'Place that picture down so you can't see it and get a fresh sheet of paper. Focus on that issue again, if you were to draw a picture of how that makes you feel now, what would you draw?'

Time 1 minute.

'If your picture had a title what would the title of that picture be? Please write the title on the picture.'

'Even though I've drawn this picture and I've called it... I love and accept myself anyway.'

'And in this picture I have drawn...'

Two rounds of tapping (just body) as you look at your picture and tap on red line, blue circle, green square, black wiggles, etc.

'Place that picture down so you can't see it and get a fresh sheet of paper.'

Continue until all participating are resolved.

Or if after picture 4 anyone is not ready for the resolution picture, for picture 5:

'Draw a picture of what you would draw when this issue has been resolved.'

Resolution picture.

'If you were to put a frame around this picture where your issue has been resolved what colour would that frame be?'

Reimprint

Close your eyes and imagine flooding the frame colour through your body in any way that feels right to you, so that every fibre of your being is saturated with that colour, every cell in your body is singing the song of that colour, every fibre of your being is dancing the dance of that colour – especially any areas that hold pain or emotion. Take as long as you like and tell me when it is done.'

STT – SILENT TAPPING TECHNIQUE

This is a technique that is particularly beneficial in school. Children come in with whatever they may have experienced at home, anger and anxiety picked up from parents and siblings in particular. They also absorb things they hear on the news, online and from friends. During the school day there are many situations which can potentially cause anxiety, namely transitions during classroom change, subject change, moving from playground to classroom, classroom to hall and so on. In the book 'Do the Nattylala' written by Phil Reed and Annie Moodliar, you can read in detail about an experiment carried out in a school where they introduced tapping at different times throughout the day. Children quickly started to use it spontaneously as they needed it and others joined in. It was used as a behaviour management technique where they had used clapping before to get everyone focused and quiet.

It is basically EFT tapping but in silence, where all the same tapping points are used but not words, because each child is encouraged to focus on their own feelings.

The technique is introduced to the children and you can use the EFT explanation given earlier in this chapter. Whether they believe it will help or not does not actually matter, it will work anyway!

Everyone tapping together will help too. This is called 'borrowing the benefits'.

Exercise

The teacher starts the process at registration by starting to tap on the karate chop point. Children join in with the tapping in silence. Once everyone is tapping on the karate chop point, you can start moving through the tapping points, slowly reminding children of the steps so they do a round of tapping for each step.

Step 1 – Notice how you feel, pay attention to your feelings.

Step 2 – Accept the negative feelings because they are just a part of us, we can love ourselves and still not like the bad feelings. Accepting ourselves 'warts and all' is important in this process. We are not our feelings just as we are not our thoughts.

Step 3 – Breathe deeply in for 4 and out for 4 as you tap around your points. This helps calm the body and the mind and prepare you for a great learning state having released the negative energy.

Step 4 – Notice any remaining negative feelings and allow yourself to let them go.

Step 5 – Breathe again, in for 4 and out for 4 as you return to the tap around the points.

Step 6 – Tapping on the karate chop point again. Notice how much calmer you feel and how you have done this yourself, and how you have managed your own emotions.

Encourage them to use this skill whenever they need to and talk about when they'd like to do it during the school day. Many children find it so helpful that they share it with their family.

FINALLY

Although I've described EFT and PTT here in sufficient detail for you to use them with clients and children you care for, it is recommended that you take the full training to get the full understanding of the science behind them and learn variations on the EFT technique that you can use with specific issues such as chronic pain, allergies, and PTSD. The techniques I have described will work for the majority of cases, but when you do the training, you will have more options. Also, it will be beneficial to extend your training to include Matrix Reimprinting which enables you to take your client back to their first six years and address the core belief at the time they imprinted it. Other training courses will enable you to rebirth your client or their child (Matrix Birth Reimprinting) or even go back to a past life (Matrix Past Life Reimprinting). As it is impossible to publish up to date course information, please get in touch with me to discuss your training requirements and I'll give you further details.

(5)

THE HEALING POWER OF ART

I use a lot of art in my work. Children love to draw and paint and express themselves through their creativity. It is not a new idea; indeed they were using art to gain insight into the child's deeper world as far back as the 1940s. As a Qualitative Market Researcher trained by Bill Schlackman in the 1970s, we used drawing and pictures to avoid asking direct questions and to get a more in-depth response to advertising material.

'The overall consensus is that art expressions are uniquely personal statements that have elements of both conscious and unconscious meaning in them, and can be representative of many different aspects of the children who create them.' [Cathy A Malchiodi – Understanding Children's Drawings]

A child's drawing is just that: a drawing. It cannot be right or wrong. There can be no judgement. Indeed, I find that by having paper, felt pens, paints and crayons, glitter and other creative materials on the table makes it the first thing they see when we start work together, and is something unexpected and fun. This is their world, the world of cutting and sticking, drawing and creating. Sometimes I find my students reluctant about art therapy. They have trained in NLP, perhaps with someone who focuses more on the adult world, and they wonder how they can connect NLP and art. I can assure you that when a child is drawing you can observe their patterns and processes in a way that simply isn't the case when you ask direct questions.

Children cannot easily articulate their emotions, perceptions or beliefs, but by combining their drawing and their verbal descriptions together with observation, you will get good rapport and understanding.

Before they come to us they will have been asked, 'What's wrong?' and tried to explain and perhaps been asked why they feel like that and they don't know. Then they feel stupid because they can't explain why, and they genuinely don't know. Part of the reason for this is that the core belief that has been triggered was imprinted in utero, in the first six years of their life, or could even be ancestral. What occurred at that time was what we call a UDIN – it was *unexpected, dramatic, isolating* and for which they had *no strategy*. In that moment, the small child goes into 'freeze mode' because they are shocked and can neither fight nor flight. They may have no conscious recollection of the event nor of what they made it mean, yet the core belief is imprinted and continues to trigger every time they experience a similar event. In effect, they attract the situation because their subconscious is on the lookout for it. Is it any wonder, then, that it needs a different technique, a non-talking technique to access this early memory? Using art which connects so readily with their child self, and which has no logic or overt communication, their subconscious connects and communicates what it feels.

Often my client has no understanding of why they've drawn what they've drawn, and they don't need to know. When they talk about their picture or, in the case of PTT, tap on their picture, the healing happens at this deeper level.

Our role is simply to provide the materials and help them with taking tops off, opening jars, etc., observing and supporting them silently during the process, then providing a safe space for them to tell you about their drawing.

Many students find it surprising that we don't need to know anything about the event, situation, issue or have any explanations. In this sense I love art therapy because it remains so true to the intention of NLP that everyone already has the resources. This therapy is child-led. They do the work and they do the healing. We are simply the conduit. We hold the space, using simple repetitive questioning to keep them connected to their subconscious, silent during much of the process and observing. I like to match their breathing and occasionally take a deeper breath which they tend to match as we're in rapport. This breath work encourages energetic shifts and promotes healing and energy moves around the body. I will often also use an essential oil in the diffuser, something gentle and relaxing like Serenity or Frankincense. There are some lovely emotional blends too that I like to use like Console or Forgive.

The language of the subconscious mind is image and colour; it is not words. Whether the child just draws lines and squiggles, the colours they choose, how they do it, what they ask and how they describe what they've drawn, is their story. By putting it out there on paper or in a sand tray, they can distance themselves from it, make those feelings safer and under their control. We want children to understand that it is not them who is the problem, the problem is the problem, and we can help them resolve it.

From 'The secret world of Drawings' by Gregg M Firth, I want to share his list of what to look for in children's (indeed anyone's) drawings.

o First impressions
o Size of the drawing in relation to the size of the paper
o The feeling being conveyed
o What's odd?
o Any barriers, who or what is blocking who or what
o What is missing?
o What is central?
o Any shape distortion
o Repeated objects
o Perspective
o Shading
o Hedging – something half in/out of the picture
o Underlining
o Erasings
o Words in drawings to add definition

PROCESS

1. Having set the task, I sit and watch, noting the above list only mentally as I don't want my client to feel judged. Although they should be aware that this is part of the therapy and isn't simply drawing a tree or a flower, for example. It is not a 'picture' as such and won't tell a story of a situation or an issue but will, in its own way, encapsulate the feeling of it. I'll just say, 'Tell me when you're finished,' and I usually pre-frame that I'm looking for a 'top of the mind' expression so they have about 5 minutes and they can use any of the coloured felt pens (make sure you have black).

2. I will then sit back in my chair to break state. I want to convey that this is a different stage and one of reflection, curiosity and non-judgement. The 'doing' part has been done and now we're wondering and 'being' with the drawing. I may say, 'Tell me about your drawing,' or, 'What is going on in this picture?'

3. I like some of Malchiodi's questions and will use these:

    a. How do the people or animals in this picture feel?

    b. How does the shape or colour feel?

    c. How do the figures in the drawing feel about each other?

    d. If they could speak, what would they say to each other?

    e. Can I ask the little boy/little girl something? (using the third person can sometimes move things a bit deeper as it feels safer being non direct, giving a sense of safety). I might use a glove puppet or finger puppet to answer the question, 'Would you like to use one of these puppets to talk?'

    f. 'What would they do if they could move?'

4. Keep their drawings, they should not go home as they are part of the therapy process and are confidential material from the client session.

If you have a new client and want an easy first drawing, here are some ideas;

o Me
o Me and my family

- Me and my friends
- Me and my pet
- Me and my house
- Favourite things I like to do

I have a set of Art Therapy Cards from Elitsa Velikova and I use these a lot. I love the ideas and her suggested questions. I'd love to be able to say that I add some of my own questions but I don't because hers are so good.

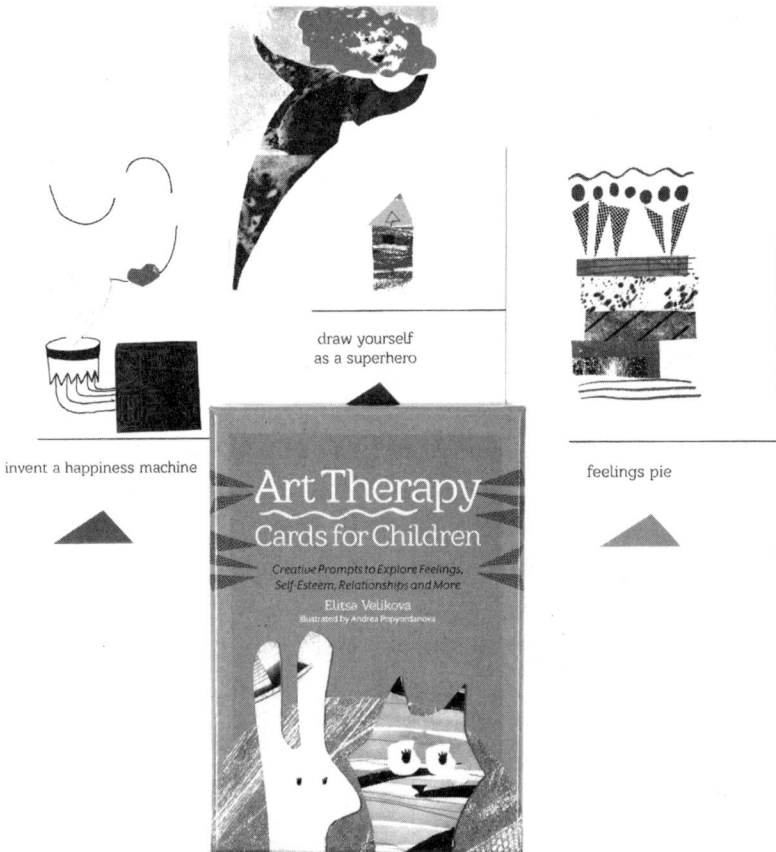

draw yourself
as a superhero

invent a happiness machine

feelings pie

Art Therapy
Cards for Children

*Creative Prompts to Explore Feelings,
Self-Esteem, Relationships and More*

Elitsa Velikova
Illustrated by Andrea Popyordanova

Here are some I would recommend:

1.   What is inside the body?

This is a great introduction to talking about feelings. I draw an outline of a body and ask my client:

'Tell me some of the feelings you get.'

They are most likely to tell you the feelings they get most often as these will be top of mind. They write the feeling down, say 'sadness'. Ask them to give it a colour using the felt pens, putting a solid circle of that colour next to the word.

Then I ask them to use that colour to show where in their body they feel that feeling. Often there will be several places. They may tell you when they feel that feeling but I prefer to just leave this as a feelings exercise with no discussion in order to keep them out of their conscious mind because I don't want them to feel they have to explain their feelings or justify them.

Go through the feelings they mention, assigning them a colour and place in the body.

I find this a good way to introduce tapping to them as they now realise that their feelings are in the body.

Elitsa also includes exercises called Feelings Map and Feelings Pie and I've done both of these. They are similar in concept to the body one above, allowing the child to talk about their feelings in a creative way.

When using the The Feelings Pie, I often do the exercise like a recipe. I ask them to say how much of each feeling they have in their body(pie) and they draw their body like a pie or a cake and use different colours to fill in how much of each feeling they have.

2.   The happiness machine

This is truly one of my favourite exercises and I frequently do it using LEGO. I use LEGO Serious Play because it contains all the different colour bricks and lots of intriguing and different pieces that help children use their imagination. It is important not to use any LEGO figures as they are making a metaphor and not trying to recreate reality in LEGO.

This exercise can of course also be done using felt pens and paper or other construction materials.

Give your client your LEGO tin/box and ask them to create a happiness machine.

I love Elitsa's questions:

o What is it called?
o How does it work?
o Who starts it?
o Who is it for?
o When would they use it?
o Where would they use it?
o What would your life be like if you had this machine?
o What would your family's life be like if you had this machine?
o How would life at school be like if you had this machine?

I ask about the colours too, using clean language, for example, 'Tell me about the blue, what does blue mean for you?'

This exercise leads naturally on to a discussion about when they need it, when they're sad, what makes them sad, and through creating their own 'happiness machine' they are introduced to the concept that they have the ability to change their own feelings and understand the process of how this 'machine' works.

3.   Draw yourself as a superhero

Who doesn't want to draw themselves as a superhero?

This is a great, fun exercise, and like all the other drawing and creative tasks, this is a way of getting to understand your child client. Having said, 'child client' remember that I mean all ages from 4yrs – 21yrs, and mums and dads too! Getting into our inner child is a very healing place to be, especially for adults.

This would usually be a drawing exercise using felt pens and, again, I would recommend using Elitsa's questions.

o   What is his/her name?
o   What are their superpowers and what can they do with them?
o   What other skills do they have?
o   Who are they designed for?
o   Does the hero have a special mission?
o   What is the special suit? (I will use clean questions to ask about the colours of each item of their clothing)
o   Where does the hero live? (I often ask them to draw where they live as well)
o   Do they have a trusted buddy or assistant? (Draw them too)
o   What are the personality traits of the hero? What are their personal qualities?
o   Do you have these in you as well?
o   Are there any qualities in this hero that you would like to develop in yourself?

Example

I did this exercise yesterday with a new seven-year-old client who was anxious about Coronavirus. The government had just announced that schools may be returning and there was a lot of anxiety around this and about how children would have to be split up so that social distancing could be maintained. His mother had explained that he was unable to express his emotions. When asked how he felt, he said he didn't feel anything. She said she observed that he felt frustrated and angry and that he didn't like change.

My client's superhero was dressed in a white suit and wore a red sash. He was a Japanese kickboxer who could kick bad people out of the way. He was lightning-fast so he could catch bad people, and he was very skilled at what he did because he practised a lot. He lived in Japan and travelled on public transport like a normal person. He didn't like using his superpowers, but sometimes he got overwhelmed and he had to use them to protect the city from bad people, or when bad things happened.

Now, here's how we can link into NLP anchoring. He said the skill he would like to develop was being able to stand up to people but he sometimes feels shy. So this is where I would introduce anchoring.

I asked, 'How could you use that red sash to remind you to be brave and confident so you could speak out?'

He said that he could touch it so he could be 'brave like fire'. Then he said that his superhero had other sashes. He had a green sash for earth, for when he wanted to 'empty himself of stress', a white one for air, for remembering things and feeling calm, and a blue one which was his normal sash for being kind and loyal 'because I am not always loyal'. He had said that his hero was an only child (he has a sister and they don't get on very well as there was a lot of resentment from her at the attention he had as a baby).

We then talked about when he would use each 'anchor' and touch the sash and its specific colour. He said he would touch the white sash at night time, the green sash for remembering and the red sash 'when seeing someone you don't want to see and for feeling confident'.

Using this simple drawing exercise (online) I was able to have a very productive first session and he was able to express feelings in a safe way because he wasn't being asked directly about them.

Other drawing exercises I regularly do are:

o Paint a dream
o Family tree collage
o Safe place
o Yourself

4. Sand Tray

This is another favourite. I have a perfect inflatable sand tray and a Tupperware container of pink sand, a box of sea creatures, dinosaurs, moulds, shells and moshi monsters. I like to use this for a face-to-face first session. It is my interpretation of the NLP belief of excellence – 'the map is not the territory'.

I ask the child to use the materials to create their own world: their home, mum's or dad's home if their parents don't live together, school, any other aspects of their life that are important. They can use any of the pieces for themselves, family members, school friends and so on.

I leave them to do this on their own of course and don't interfere or ask questions as they do it. I notice how they do it, in which order, what they change, how they approach the task, the questions they ask, and so on.

Then I ask them to describe their world.

I use clean questions for each item:

o Tell me about this
o What is there about that?
o Anything about the size of this
o Anything about where you've placed that
o You changed this a few times, what was going on there?
o You took this away, tell me about that?
o You added this here, tell me about that?
o What about this (colour)?
o What does (colour) mean to you?
o Where are you in this world you've created?

Notice their language patterns as they describe their sand tray. You should be able to determine their dominant patterns. Be on the watch for 'away from' thinking, for 'mismatching', 'external referencing' and so on. Notice any 'victim' language, who is the rescuer and perpetrator?

Then I take some photos of the sand tray, maybe some close ups of specific areas of it such as their home or school.

The second part of the session speaks more to 'compelling outcomes'.

'You've just created your world as it is to you. Now I'd like you to recreate it as you'd like it to be. This is called our 'compelling outcome'. Knowing what we want is the first step to getting it. Creating it piece by piece connects to the neural pathways in our brain, preparing it for this change.'

Now your client can recreate their world. Notice what they change, what they remove, what they add, and notice how their physiology changes as they make these changes. Their body will shift, their energy will move. They will be more upright, more connected and engaged in the task, and their mood will be lighter as their mind connects to this more positive outcome. They are taking responsibility for change, it is in their hands, literally.

At the end, just ask if there's anything more they want to change, there probably will be. They just needed that extra push.

Again, ask your list of questions but as it's about compelling outcomes, I tend to use a more hypnotic style of questioning such as 'I'm wondering...'

We need to keep them focused on 'towards thinking' what they want, although this is much easier for them having now created that compelling outcome. It's fine if they want to make more changes as they speak, in fact, I find they often do, as they tweak their outcome, making it better and better. Remember, this reinforces the feeling for them that they are responsible for their outcome, no one else.

I take photos and these will probably be our starting point for the next session, where we will look at the skills they have for achieving this outcome, and then we will move on to overcoming any limiting beliefs.

VISUAL EXPLORER CARDS AND VISION BOARDS

I have a set of four packs of Visual Explorer cards and use them frequently as a way for clients to explore their identity, their deeper needs and intentions, and to create a talking point that connects with who they really are, beyond gender, age and so on.

By using metaphor, image, colour, we can learn so much more about what our client needs and wants in their life than simply by asking them. So often these are things they just don't know. Did we know at their age? Probably not.

I use them in different ways.

Exercise

Lay out the cards on the table, so your client can rummage through them. There are a lot of cards! Trust that they will be drawn to ones that resonate in some way. I ask them to draw out:

o *Any that they love*
o *Any that they hate*
o *Ones that inspire them*
o *Ones that make them sad*

You can focus on identity and ask them to pull out any that remind them of themselves in some way.

Focus on a compelling outcome perhaps, pick cards that reflect what they want out of life. This can be really helpful for working with teenagers.

When they've picked their cards, go through each one using clean language questions

o Tell me about this one
o What is there about this card?

Then I tend to group them in their sets relating to the task I've given them so we can then look at patterns. They will notice a connection between the cards they've chosen that they love or hate or are inspired by. I take photos for my records and they often like to do the same. I've had teenage clients create a screensaver, home screen or similar, to work as visual affirmations of who they are or who they want to be.

In family sessions, this exercise can be a great talking point as children discover things they didn't know about their parents.

You can also use it when talking about modelling excellence, looking at those cards that inspire them in some way, you can ask them how they are like this in some part of their life.

Their choice of cards will also reflect their values and beliefs and it can be very helpful for teenagers in particular to have the opportunity to use metaphor as a way to understand who they are and what matters to them as they start to make their way to University and a chosen career. I've had quite a few seventeen-year-olds who have just found themselves at the point of choosing a university course and realised they had no idea what they wanted to do in life, who they are and what was important to them, because they'd just been through the academic process, taking tests but not looking at the bigger picture of what it was all for.

LEGO SERIOUS PLAY

I use LEGO a lot. We make LEGO models of

o Happiness
o Friendship
o Success
o My family
o Fear

I've used it for Picture Tapping (see EFT and PTT chapter) and also to help us with the Logical Levels of Change.

I use Lego as an alternative to drawing, some children prefer it. Funnily enough, the ones it works least well with are those who are mad keen on Lego because they think of making a model of a specific thing. Here we are using Lego as metaphor so we use the pieces we are drawn to rather than the ones we need to make a model of a ship or whatever.

Example

I worked with a twelve-year-old boy some months ago and he was fearful of failure. It could be any failure: exams, football, friendships.

His first model of fear of failure had a lot of black bricks and was quite unstable.

We did a round of tapping.

He added other colours and we tapped on anger because he was annoyed with himself for having this fear which frequently debilitated him.

We tapped again.

Then he added some wheels to make his model more stable but he still felt that he was held back and limited by his fears.

We tapped again.

Now he took off a few pieces of Lego and made it more streamlined and he added a flag.

We reimprinted this model of success using the colour he chose to represent the new skills he had to overcome his fears.

We tap on each brick colour, each part of the model at each stage:

4 red bricks
one window
one long grey bit

...and so on. The thing is that they know why they've chosen that piece, we don't need to know. We can ask about the colour:

'Tell me about the red, what does red mean to you?'

We can ask about the number:

'Is there anything about the <u>four</u> red bricks?'

Sometimes there can be a link between the number of bricks used of a particular colour and the age they were when that belief, say fear of failure, was imprinted. It's quite remarkable what we hold in our subconscious mind, that is released by creativity.

CRYSTAL TIME LINE

I have a bag of crystals which I pour out onto the table, children find these fascinating and like to feel them and touch them. They are different colours and textures, sizes and opacity. You can buy these quite easily or gather a collection of something similar such as shells.

Exercise

I might ask them to choose one that represents themselves. Obviously they are not a crystal so they are projecting their own characteristics and identity onto the crystal and describing how they feel they are like that. This yields great insight and allows the child complete freedom to choose how to describe themselves.

I then ask them to choose other crystals for Mum, Dad, siblings and friends. It is interesting to hear them describe the people in their world and it gives me a better idea than if they simply said 'I have a sister and her name is... she is x years of age.'

Exercise

My favourite exercise with crystals is to make what I call a 'Crystal Time Line'. I ask them to think about their current school year and choose a crystal to represent it. I then ask them to look at the crystal they've chosen and tell me how it reflects that school year.

Then we take the previous school year, the one before and so on until we get back to nursery and then birth and before. It's amazing how children can guess which crystal represents them in utero. Using crystals gives them permission to be creative and guess because obviously they weren't a crystal so in the guesswork is their access to their subconscious mind.

When we then look at the line of the crystals on the paper and the words written alongside each one, a pattern emerges and we can clearly see where there were traumas or UDINs, times when they imprinted a belief that affected that year and perhaps subsequent years. We can see colours of crystals, noting the choice of darker ones, smaller ones, more solid ones.

This is often an exercise I do early on in my work with a child to explore what we need to work on.

THE LANGUAGE OF COLOUR

Colour has a vibration and we can use it to access the subconscious mind, understand our children and what they need without asking direct questions. This is always my goal, ever since my years in Market Research running focus groups with children.

You only need to think about how we feel in the winter surrounded by the dark colours and the lack of light. Then in the spring as the beautiful yellow daffodils and spring flowers emerge, the green shoots of new life, new beginnings, our soul sings.

Colour brings up emotions. Our eyes, circulatory system, nervous system and digestive system are all affected by colour. It is the language of our subconscious mind and is readily accessed. We instinctively know the colour of our emotions and the colour we need to bring in to lift and lighten it.

Exercise

Ask your child to draw something they fear or something that makes them feel uncomfortable. It may be a spider for example, I have helped lots of children with a fear of spiders. The chances are that they will use black and make the spider very scary looking.

Now ask them what colours they need to add to take away that scary feeling. They will add yellow or pink. They will add eyelashes, a smile, a funny hat or something to make it seem more fun.

The same creative powers they use to make a spider scary, they can also use to make it friendly. It's all in the mind.

As coaches, therapists, or practitioners, think about the colours you wear. Dark colours absorb energy so you will pick up your client's energy. Instead wear light colours to reflect it back. Blue is a great colour for communication which is obviously good in any work with children and teens. I love wearing blue and my therapy room is blue and looks out onto the garden which is very green, the colour of the heart chakra.

Notice the colours your client wears, the colours your child loves to wear. What do they tell you?

What colours do you need to wear for you to feel connected to your world and at your best?

Parents, think about the colours you use in the children's bedroom. Red will energise, motivate and could trigger anger whereas green will be more about harmony and balance so would be a better colour for somewhere they sleep.

There is a science around colour and its vibration. When we know the colours connected to the energy centres in the body, this helps us to understand the emotions connected to each colour.

Top of the head/crown chakra – violet – spiritual connection or higher purpose

Centre of the forehead/third eye – indigo – intuition or insight

Throat – blue – speaking your truth or being heard

Heart – green – relationships and emotional balance

Stomach – yellow – personal power, identity, ego

Lower stomach area – sacral – orange – sexuality, creativity, trauma

Base of spine – red – survival, material world, money worries

I haven't any experience of using art therapy with specific groups, such as selective mutes, or children who speak a different language, but both I would expect to find some release by being able to express their emotions through art.

6

HOW TO TURN 'COMPARING' INTO 'MODELLING EXCELLENCE'
NLP MODELLING PROCESS

Modelling is what makes NLP different from other modalities. The premise is that when you find a model of excellence for a task, skill, quality or whatever you have observed in someone you admire, by copying the structure of the skill and obtaining and inculcating the belief behind the skill, you too can have it.

Modelling is invaluable as it enables us to acquire whatever skills and qualities we see in others, and, wait for it... in ourselves too! Yes, the chances are that in some part of our life and our world we have the very thing we have noticed in someone else and so admire. In fact, as you'll remember from an earlier chapter, this is one of the presuppositions of NLP – if you spot it, you've got it.

My own NLP Trainer, Sue Knight, describes it perfectly:

> *'When we step into someone else's shoes and reproduce what they do and the results they achieve, we are modelling.'*

As does Jeremy Lazarus who trained me as an NLP Sport Practitioner:

> *'In modelling we elicit the strategies, beliefs, values and fundamental filters and the physiology that allows someone to produce certain behaviour. Then we codify these in a series of steps designed to make the behaviour easy to reproduce.'*

What we are doing when we model someone is to observe their behaviour patterns and be curious about how they achieve their results and how they do that differently from someone who doesn't. In NLP we refer to *the difference that makes the difference.* For this we need a blank sheet of paper, we need to set aside our own guesswork and assumptions. This is much easier for children to do than adults. We, as adults tend to say, 'Oh, I tried that, and it didn't work,' or, 'That isn't possible,' or 'I can't do that'. In effect, we need to believe that when we understand the thinking patterns and the behaviours used by our model of excellence, then we can do that too.

You might well say that this is exactly how you learn and tell me that you still can't achieve that great result but – and this is the NLP part – have you truly identified the belief of your model of excellence? The problem is that people who do a thing well often don't themselves know what their belief is. They may guess and the chances are that they are wrong. They have found that skill easy to acquire, maybe they have been able to do that thing for years. The belief is so well ingrained in their subconscious that it has become second nature, so when you ask them what it is, they go to their conscious brain and out pops some logical explanation of the underlying belief. But when you take on that belief, it doesn't work for you. This is why we may seek out a number of models of excellence for the skill. Some people are better able to dig deep and be curious in order to help you.

So what have we learnt here?

Sometimes you'll find the belief of excellence can be found before the thing you're modelling is even started, other times it will be at a specific point in the process. You will always find that somewhere in your own life you have this belief that you need for the new skill, but you may have to be very curious because it might not be obvious where it is.

Imagine you have something you need to do but you are someone who tends to get distracted by social media, or you simply have too many other jobs to do and keep putting it off. In order to get this task done you'd need to learn from someone who can focus without being distracted, so first you need to find a few people who can do this really well.

Example

I remember one of my students wanting to model the way another student (who happened to be heavily pregnant at the time) did a yoga headstand. So Julia demonstrated the pose against a door in my home. She did it elegantly and slowly so Nic could see each part of the pose. This way, Nic was able to learn the structure, but when she tried to do it, she just bunny-hopped her legs up and they just came back down again. So we knew that something was happening at that point in the manoeuvre to stop her. What was it?

She tried again.

The same thing happened.

I asked, 'What goes through your head at that point when your legs come back down?'

'I can't do it,' she said.

So I asked Julia what her belief was at that point.

'There isn't a step at that point,' she said.

Interesting. For our model of excellence it was one move, but for Nic there were two moves.

I then asked Julia what her belief was when she was standing there about to do it.

She said, 'This is a fun thing to do.'

I asked Nic what her belief was at that point. It was: 'I won't be able to do this.'

So how could we switch the limiting belief of Nic's to the resourceful belief of excellence that Julia had?

I asked Nic to think of something she thought of as being a fun thing to do and she thought about playing with her small children. We anchored that. She tried it again.

Success!

Check out your friends and colleagues. Study their form. What is their pattern? What can you learn just through observation? Can you find any interviews with them or any articles where they are talking about their skills and qualities, tips for success, habits and advice?

You need to find out what they are thinking. You need to find out their values and beliefs about getting things done by the deadline. What's different in their thinking that leads to a 'get it done now' attitude rather than procrastinating, which is what you do (in my example). Follow them on Twitter and ask the question directly there or send a direct message. Check their Instagram feed and see what you notice.

You can discover their thinking and underlying beliefs by asking them directly: 'What's important to you about getting things done?' and then go through the structure again with this answer and way of thinking in your mind.

You can also think about your own life. Is there an area of your life where you don't, in fact, procrastinate and you are fully active? We don't behave the same in all situations. Perhaps in sport, or at home or work there may be something you do with focus, determination and speed. Imagine you're doing that now.

....

....

....

....

What's the underlying belief about why you're doing this like this?

....

....

....

It may surprise you to learn that modelling those who do things that really annoy you can also be very rewarding. One of the NLP presuppositions is 'if you spot it, you've got it' which loosely means, in the context of modelling anyway, that if something is annoying you, there's potentially something to be learned there!

Example

Marie was so annoyed at the way her husband used to fold all the laundry after it had finished tumble drying. Particularly annoying was his folding technique which was apparently time-consuming and precise. Marie felt that it was overly fastidious and an unnecessary waste of time.

She modelled him as per our lesson and at our next meeting she complained how annoying and pointless a homework it had been. I then asked where such a model could potentially prove useful and she 'got it'.

'I am incredibly careless and often misplace notes I've made from client calls then try and find them when they are due for their appointment. I sometimes even have people turn up and I hadn't put their appointment in my diary. This model of attention to detail will actually be very useful in my business.'

I hope she stopped giving her hubby a tough time over his folding after this realisation!

Example

Donna modelled her young son because he really annoyed her by ignoring her calls for supper because he was so engrossed in his Minecraft games. She also couldn't see the point of doing something she found annoying. 'I don't want to play computer games!' she protested.

Nevertheless, she sat down beside him and learned how to do Minecraft and actually surprised herself by how addictive it could be. It sounded as if her son also enjoyed teaching his mother, especially as she'd been so dismissive of the game prior to this point.

Anyway at our next session she confessed that she'd enjoyed the process of modelling and had understood how absorbing and enjoyable it could be and how much more preferable, to a young boy, than coming to supper. But initially she could not see how such a model could be useful to her. Then she got it!

> *'I've been trying to complete my PhD in Child Psychology but, every time I sit down to write it, I get distracted and find myself doing something else. With this model of 100% focus and not even hearing anything else, I can finish my thesis.'*
>
> *And she did!*

So in a nutshell, whether you model someone who does something you want to be able to do and admire and are inspired by or whether you model someone doing something very annoying in order to extract their belief and apply it elsewhere in your life, it's up to you.

Once you understand how to model for yourself, you will be able to help your young clients and parents do the same. Children naturally compare themselves to their peers and through modelling you can get them to learn how to be confident by modelling the most confident child in their class, be the best at maths or English, score more goals and so on. Crucially, they can also model their own excellence because they will already have the belief they need in some other part of their life. Here's a really good example of that:

Example
One of my young clients, Josh, was struggling to make friends. Let's look at what skills are involved in this process:

- o *Deciding who to approach*
- o *Going up to them*
- o *Having something to say*
- o *Responding to what they say*
- o *Repeating the process with others*

Where might Josh have these skills?
Yes – in sport!
I asked him to talk me through how he played rugby.

> *'I look for the ball, grab it and look to see who's free. I give him the eye to let him know he's to catch it. I then run ahead, make myself free and he passes back to me or to someone else if they're free or in a better position.'*
>
> *This isn't verbatim as it was a year or so ago and I can't remember exactly what he said so apologies if my rugby terminology isn't great. However, the gist was that some decision was taken about who to approach and the ball was passed and caught so this meant that a communication took place. Using this as a metaphor for making friends was quite an easy step for Josh to see that in fact he did have the skills he needed, he just needed to transfer them to a different area of his life.*

He had a limiting belief about his ability to make friends but a resourceful belief about communicating on the sports field.

Take this belief and apply it to where you need it.

When modelling, it is extremely important to select models who are not only excellent exemplars of the skill but also people who will be willing and able to explain their underlying beliefs and values. Many gifted and skilled people may be unable to get in touch with their feelings and even less able to express them in a way that you can understand and use. In order for us to replicate the model of excellence we must take on their beliefs. It is much easier than you think to take on someone's belief, and it starts by saying to yourself 'What if I believed this?' and then acting as if you do. Once we have their structure and beliefs we can start thinking about the values they must have that underpin them. We test out our hypotheses by repeating what we have observed and taking on the beliefs and values. One by one we remove different elements to find out which parts of our model are the ones we need to replicate the excellence. Then we have our model which we can teach to others. The proof of how successfully we have modelled will lie in the ability to pass it on to others who can then get the same result.

I wonder who your models of excellence would be...

Exercise

I want to model the way ....

does..

Imagine all the amazing skills you will learn!

⑦

SPEAKING SO THEY LISTEN
VAK AND THE
METAPROGRAMMES

On the whole, child clients do tend to listen to practitioners, coaches and teachers, so this chapter is probably more for parents. Parent readers may also work with other people's children so they do know that they are listened to, just not by their own children.

This is an important point. Do you find that you are listened to at work but not at home?

I'm guessing the answer to that question is 'Yes!' because I've heard it a thousand times and experienced it myself on a daily basis.

Would you believe me if I told you that you speak differently at work to how you speak to the kids?

Let me take you back to the chapter on Modelling. Remember that we already have the resources (beliefs of excellence) and we can model our own excellence which, in this case, will be how we communicate at work. Can you imagine our colleagues ignoring us as our children do, or answering back or shouting? No, of course not. This is because there is respect, a little fear of the consequences, and also very little emotional investment. When we speak, we expect them to listen, and they know this and do so. They know and accept that if they do not, then there would be consequences.

How about when we speak to our children and teens. Are there consequences? Yes, there are, but what will usually happen is that instead of speaking so they listen, we speak expecting them *not* to listen, so they don't. We cannot *not* communicate. The tone of our voice, our posture, and the words we use clearly communicate that we don't expect them to listen. Often, we'll shout from somewhere else in the house. Would we do this at work? I think not! We may not get eye contact before speaking or ask if now is a good time to talk as we might do at work.

It comes down to our belief. When we model how we talk at work we need to instil that belief about ourselves at the same time.

'I have something important to say.'

'I deserve to be heard.'

'You must listen to me.'

'I am important.'

'There will be consequences if you don't pay attention.'

So the first thing to think about when you address this issue of speaking so they listen is: 'Who am I when I'm speaking to my children?' Most of the time it may not matter whether they listen or not, so you can relax, but when you <u>do</u> need them to pay attention, you need to actively morph into work mode.

The second thing to think about is that if they still don't listen then they are being disrespectful. It does not mean that you are a useless mum or dad, or that you are a failure, or that they will turn into hooligans!

Here you are deleting, generalising and distorting.

Generalisations are when we use words like; always, everyone, never, no one, every and so on. Generalisations are rarely if ever true, and so if you say this to them they will just ignore it because it simply isn't correct.

'You never listen to me.'

'I always have to remind you to brush your teeth.'

'No-one plays with me at school.'

'I've got no friends.'

'All the teachers pick on me.'

When faced with a generalisation from your child or client, notice it. There is an attention-seeking element, so give it some attention by using a 'clean language' question rather than arguing that what they say can't possibly be true. Here are some good options;

o Repeat the generalisation back as a question
   – 'never?'
   – 'always?'
   – 'non-one?'
   – 'no friends?'
   – 'all?'

This is a gentle way to acknowledge what they've said, point out the generalisation and be available for them to talk about their feelings.

Instead of generalising, it's more helpful to focus on the exceptions, so think about those times when you <u>are</u> listened to and use this as your model of excellence. It will be at work, yes, but also there will be the occasional time when your family does pay attention. What was the structure of that model of excellence? You may well find that it was when you spoke calmly, gave eye contact and asked them with plenty of time to spare, not at the last minute so they could finish what they were doing first.

Did you *delete* the context?

This is another example of vague language and there are several examples of ways we do this.

1. Comparisons.

How often do we say to our child or client, 'that's much better' or, 'you've done that well' but there is no context for the comparison and this makes it hard for them to apply the feedback. They are left wondering 'how is it better?' or 'better than whom?' or 'better than last week?', 'better than my brother/sister?'

We make comparisons ourselves and this is the first step for modelling. We can begin by saying 'she is better than me at maths' and then 'chunk down'. This means that we go in search of the context that is missing.

o Better? How?
o In what way? What does she do that is better?
o How does she do it?

o All Maths or just this topic we're studying now?

o What precisely does she do to get that grade?

o How could I do that too and get that grade?

o I wonder what her belief is about her ability to get a good grade in this topic?

Do you see how we've moved from a fairly meaningless vague comparison to a useful modelling exercise?

2. Nominalisations

When children say they have 'anxiety' or 'anger issues' these are examples of 'nominalisations' because they are describing how they feel using one word that could mean something different to everyone who uses it.

o What exactly do they experience?

o When? Is it every time?

o With someone specifically?

o Where do they feel it?

o What happens?

o What happens next?

o How is it resolved?

In many ways I feel that labels such as ADHD, Autism, Dyslexia and so on are also nominalisations because it assumes everyone using that word, experiences the same symptoms. Instead, in NLP, we tend to focus on tackling the barriers to what children want by helping them overcome their limiting beliefs. Each child will have a slightly different belief based on their own early childhood and environment.

The response to nominalisations is again to 'chunk down' to the detail. Get the structure. You can then 'chunk back up' to find out what that means for them in a bigger context, how it feels to be in their map of the world.

3. Modal operators

We are all familiar with these, even if we didn't realise they had a name.

'I can't!'

Whether it's a child saying they can't do their homework or a parent saying they can't get their child to do what they've been told or a teacher feeling that they can't get the class to focus – these are all examples of being 'at effect.' When we are 'at effect' this means that we are passively accepting what we experience as being the effect of factors outside our control. However, when we take matters into our own hands, the matters we <u>can</u> control, such as our belief about our ability to do that thing, we are then 'at cause' and can change the effect.

Many teachers encourage children to add 'yet' as in 'I can't do it <u>yet</u>' which moves the phrase to 'at cause' as it adds the belief that they can and will be able to do it when they maybe read the question through again, take their time, or trust their instinct. Some children, mine included, say 'I can't do it' almost as they open their books.

A good response to a modal operator of possibility or in other words an 'I can't' is:

'...what if you could?' (accompanied by a smile and an encouraging look)

Or:

'...and if you could...?'

I quite like to add in a hypnotic embedded command like, 'I'm wondering how you'll feel when you've done it?' If you know your client or child is visual, you could say 'I'm wondering how it will look when you've done it,' and for an auditory child "I wonder what you'll say when you've done it.'

Note that we are using 'I'm wondering...' which is the hypnotic part, best accompanied by a wondering, low, slow tone for effect.

Note also that we are saying 'when' because we are assuming they will do it. Had we used 'if' instead, as in 'I'm wondering how you'll feel if you do it,' this would give them an option not to do it, which isn't the idea at all.

The answer with modal operators of possibility is to encourage possibility rather than the 'I can't' which implies that it is impossible.

Another Modal operator is that of necessity such as 'should', 'must', 'have to' and 'ought to'.

Again, we don't argue with what has been said but instead we offer up other options. A good response to any of these would be:

'What would happen if you did/did not?'

Getting our children to consider and take responsibility for the consequences of their decisions and actions is part of building emotional intelligence. Whilst we may be inclined to agree with them when they say, 'I should do my homework,' by saying 'What would happen if you did not?' will ensure they do it with a little more resolution, as the consequences (which they are aware of) would be a detention or demerit mark.

Another way that we filter what we hear, see, or feel is to *distort* it. We make it mean something based on our map of the world but this is not necessarily the same as was intended.

One I hear a lot and probably used in my pre-NLP parenting is:

'You're deliberately trying to annoy me.'
'I bet you're happy now you've made me cry.'
'You don't care what I think.'
'You won't pass your exams with that attitude to revision.'

These are all judgements and mind-reads, predictions and, as such, distortions. The response to these when someone uses them with you is to ask:

'And how exactly did I make you feel that?'

Or:

'I'm curious, how exactly did you make it mean that?'

Or:

'What evidence do you have for this?'

Or:

'How do you know that?'

It is absolutely not worth arguing because these statements are all based on a false premise that we can cause someone to feel something they do not feel or that we can predict the future. We generate our own feelings based on events and so these feelings are our choice. No one knows for sure what the future holds as we don't have full knowledge of all the factors in life, nor control over decisions impacting them.

Would we do this with our friends or colleagues? No, of course not. It would be laughable, and that is what it is here with our children as well.

Accept that in a child's map of the world, playing with LEGO or chatting to a friend on social media is much more important and enjoyable than coming to supper. Children don't deliberately want to upset their parents, it's simply a consequence of them expressing their own needs, which will often be different from ours.

Take a look at the diagram below. You'll see that the deletions, distortions and generalisations mentioned above are the first filters applied to the external event. An external event is something you see, hear or feel. We experience so many bits of information that have to be processed extremely fast, so it's only natural and essential to have an efficient filtering system operating.

When you want to improve your communication skills you need to become aware of how you filter and make what you say a more accurate reflection of what you mean. Listen for the filters your children and clients use and respond as I've suggested.

THE NLP COMMUNICATION MODEL

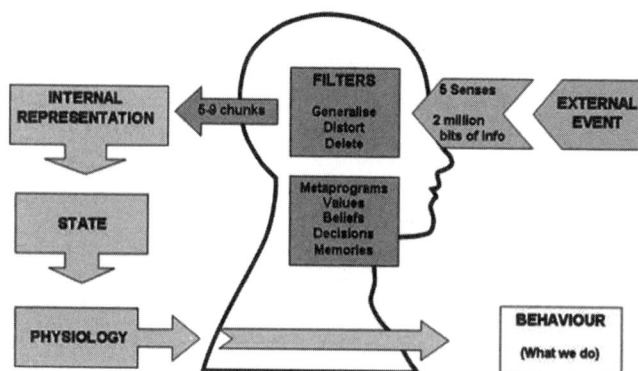

VISUAL, AUDITORY AND KINAESTHETIC

There are three internal processing preferences: visual, auditory and kinaesthetic. We have access to all of these and teachers will be skilled in teaching all children, however, we do tend to have a preference. When we want someone to listen to what we have to say, it's preferable to choose *their* preference to maximise the chances of them listening and wanting to connect with us.

A person who is *visual* will notice things they see. They will be quick to spot a change of hair style, a new dress, something having been moved to a new position in the house. They will notice colour, shape, form, texture and how you look.

They will be drawn to creative pursuits and interests. A visual child won't want to cross things out or submit work that doesn't look neat and they will enjoy subjects at school with a strong visual element, such as diagrams, colour, pictures, mind maps and other visual representations of facts.

Visual people use visual language such as:

Look
Imagine
See
Notice

Show me
Watch

When learning something new, a new language or revising for a test, learning a new process at work, visual people like to see instructions written down or write them down for themselves to refer to.

Dyslexic people are often visual, and if you have a child with this combination I would suggest you head to Olive Hickmott's website. This is her area of specialism and she trains teachers and parents in visual learning. She's also written a number of really useful books that I recommend.

Visual people tend to look up with their head and eyes as they talk because they are recalling or constructing images. They also talk fast as they try to convey the images verbally and they use a reasonably high pitch.

As a coach or teacher, think about how you can use more visual resources when working with visual children. As a parent, let them have some say in the colours in their bedroom, choosing clothes and how they like to arrange their own environment.

An *auditory* person will notice what they hear, what is said, sounds, music and all aspects of what is heard in terms of volume, pitch, tone and pace. Sounds that may not be noticed by a visual person could really irritate them, and sights that alarm a visual person they may not even be aware of. Auditory people will easily be distracted by sounds others are barely aware of. A child in a classroom sitting next to someone who is fiddling with something on their desk will be distracted and find it hard to concentrate on what the teacher is saying. Similarly, an auditory parent will be more aware of raised voices, sibling arguments and unkind words.

Words that connect with an auditory person are:

Speak
Say
Sound
Tell

Talk

Ask

Discuss

Listen

Call me

As well as being sensitive to the sound of what's being said, auditory people will remember what's said, the words and the context so they tend to be natural linguists, mimics, comics and they banter well. They are also musical and can sight read and play music from memory very well.

Because we learn to spell phonetically, they will find spelling easier than a visual person who tries to make sense of how the word looks rather than how it sounds.

Auditory people tend to speak slower than visual people – in fact, everyone speaks slower than visual people. Auditory speakers want to think about using the right word and they process a bit slower too, as they need to hear what's said and think about how they want to respond. As a parent, coach or teacher, it's helpful to allow an auditory child a bit longer to respond when asking them a question. If you are auditory and are struggling to keep up with the flow of a visual person, just ask them to slow down a bit.

Auditory learners need to have things explained slowly and clearly rather than following written instructions. If they need to read something, they will be speaking the words silently in their head.

Just as sounds and music are important to an auditory child, so is silence, and I've spoken to many an auditory child who wants to do their homework in the silence of their bedroom or with their choice of music as background rather than try to concentrate in a family room surrounded by noise they can't control.

If your child or client is *kinaesthetic* they will be quite active and physical, wanting to be close to you, touch you and will be interacting with you as much as possible. They will pick up on your mood or state of mind and pick up an atmosphere or tension, stress, and sadness much more than a visual or auditory child.

They are much more body conscious so they will feel temperature changes and be sensitive to being hot or cold. They will also be more aware of their hunger and have more specific food needs and preferences.

Kinaesthetic learners learn by doing and prefer to be doing something rather than just watching or listening. I remember once speaking at a conference about VAK (visual, auditory, kinaesthetic) and a parent put her hand up and said, 'My child told me he is kinaesthetic and therefore he wanted to learn his spelling while skateboarding!' She laughed as if this was funny.

But I asked, 'And does this work?'

'Actually it does!" she said.

It sounded as if she'd only just realised this because she had a belief that learning spellings should be done sitting at a table but this does not necessarily work best for a kinaesthetic learner. Obviously it would be difficult to have kinaesthetic learners wandering about the playground or the classroom learning, but in an ideal world each child would be able to learn as they learn best. In the meantime, they need to adapt, but this may mean that they struggle more at subjects involving static learning and excel at sport and science or subjects where they can move. A Swiss ball type chair can be helpful for them so they can keep a bit of movement going as they sit.

As a coach, I often take kinaesthetic clients outside for a walking session because I know they will be more receptive. We may walk around the garden and pick up things to make a collage when we come back inside. Favourite themes are: 'all about me', 'what makes me happy' and 'what I want to be better at'.

Speak slowly and choose words more carefully for an auditory client or child. Words that resonate with them will be:

Do
Make
Touch
Meet
Grasp
Get

Understand

Feel

Take

Children are fascinated by themselves and love to learn about why they do what they do and feel how they feel. As a therapist I pick up their preference and we talk about how this works for them and against them, what they find easy and what they struggle with. They find it enormously helpful to understand that maybe it's not them being stupid, or not understanding the lesson, but may be more about a mismatch between the teacher's preference and theirs. This might mean that they need to concentrate extra hard in those lessons or make sure they write notes in a certain way, underlining things, using colour, circling and sounding things out in their head. Knowledge is power. Once they know how they process, they can adapt accordingly. NLP is all about choices, isn't it?

When parents know their child's VAK it can make the difference between them connecting or not connecting.

Here's a simple example. Let's assume your child has a really messy room and you want them to tidy it. Think about their preferred language pattern and match it in this way.

You say:

'I've told you ten times to tidy your room, you're not listening.' (auditory)

'Just look at the state of your room, I can't see any clear carpet space at all.' (visual)

'Will you just get a move on and get that room sorted otherwise you won't be able to find anything.' (kinaesthetic)

You may be wondering how to tell which is their preferred representational system, or VAK. To some extent I find I can tell pretty early on by what the child is wearing and how they're wearing it, how they walk in, what they do, what they comment on and the questions they ask about the process I describe to them of how I work. An early chat to establish rapport will enable you to make a good guess which will start you off. I find that the metaprogrammes really reveal a child's processing patterns much more usefully and often highlight areas we will need to work on. When parents learn about these and start to notice them in their children, I find a few 'aha moments'.

When we match our child's VAK and metaprogrammes, we are in rapport, we speak the same language, so it is easy for them to listen and understand what we're saying. How we process the vast amount of information we receive through our senses creates a map of the world that is unique to us.

If you're a parent, why not write down here your own VAK and that of each of your children and perhaps your partner.

```
...............................................................................
...............................................................................
...............................................................................
...............................................................................
```

The metaprogrammes are a bit like sliding scales where we can move along the scale in either direction as a situation requires. There is no wrong end but there will be better places to be on the scale depending on what you're doing. I will explain more when we look at each scale.

Let's start with *chunk size*. This is about the amount of detail one needs in the communication. Small chunk means that your child wants the whole thing, all the details and will find being presented with the general idea overwhelming. The same would be true for the big chunk child who just needs to get a rough idea of what's happening or what they need to do, and instead you give them masses of detailed instruction. They will zone out.

One of my clients told me the other day that when her teacher explains what she has to do for homework it is in so much detail that she does just that, zones out. It's the end of the lesson and she just wants to go out and play with her friends. Then when she's at home starting her homework, she has no idea what she has to do, guesses and maybe gets it wrong. She's then in trouble. When we talked about big chunk and small chunk she suggested she has a template to use for the key pieces of information she needs – basic task, number of pages, deadline so she can listen with intent to complete it.

This is a great example of scale because we need access to both ends of the scale. We need to know what we need to do and why we need to do it but in some cases the steps may be less important. Other times the steps are very important, if for example I need to edit a document, write up notes on a client, the detail matters in the same way as it would if I'm making bread. If, however, I'm walking the dog or chatting to a friend, I can 'chunk up' and pay attention to my overall goal of having a good time.

When you're working with a child whose chunk size is small and you need them to think of the bigger picture, good questions to ask are:

o   What does that mean?
o   What's the purpose of that?
o   Where does that lead to?

If you're working with a big chunk child the questions would be:

o   How are you going to achieve that?
o   What steps do you need to take?
o   What's the first thing you need to do?

Try it on your own issues. When you're feeling overwhelmed with lots of small tasks you can chunk up to: 'what is this all for?' and when you are overwhelmed by the end goal ask yourself: 'what would be a great place to start with this?' As a writer I speak to fellow writers who get 'writers' block' and find that just writing random words on a page can be a good place to start when the task seems too big. When you're getting ground down by word count goals every day, think: what is my end goal?

The next one is *choices vs process.*

Many parents are surprised by this one. There's perceived wisdom that one should always give children choice but, quite apart from the harsh truth that we don't always get a choice in life, some children find it overwhelming.

As with chunk size, we may have a preference to have choices or not to have choices. For example, you might want a choice of what you eat at home but find choice on a menu in a new restaurant quite overwhelming.

Example

I remember a time when I visited my friend just after she'd bought a cottage she wanted to renovate. On the wall were about 20 strips of paint. They all looked white to me. She asked which she should choose, and it was important because she wanted to paint the whole house the same colour. I couldn't see enough difference to choose and found the task daunting and frustrating. I said, 'They all look the same to me,' and she said, 'Oh Judy they are all different, this one is ivory, this one is chalk, etc. etc.' Anyway, I felt completely useless and felt that I'd let her down. This is how a child can feel when faced with a choice that is of no consequence to them such as, perhaps, which vegetable or which colour mug. For another child though, that could be an important choice, and a way to express their individuality.

For those who love choices, it is important to them. It isn't necessarily about power and control, or being able to make choices and decisions. It can be about the joy of considering options and by prolonging it, meaning that they get more pleasure. Once the decision is made, that joy ceases, so they want to make it last as long as they can.

This can be annoying for a parent, particularly a 'process parent' who just wants to get things done. I've spoken to many parents who say, 'It's quite simple. They need to get in the house, take their shoes off, have a snack, do their homework, play, supper, bath and bed.' A 'choices' child resents having such a prescriptive approach and will resist. They will push against it and a parent will push back. Soon there will be shouting and stress.

However, once you realise your child likes choice, it's easy to offer them within your process.

o   What snack would you like?
o   Where would you like to do your homework?
o   Would you like squash or water?
o   Are you going to do your Maths or English first?
o   What vegetable would you like with your meal?
o   What toys would you like in the bath?
o   What story shall we read tonight?

When you do this with a process child who wants order, they will feel overwhelmed. I've actually had parents ask if their child has a problem because they can't decide between what they describe as simple choices.

However, sometimes, you do need to encourage a child to be flexible. You sometimes need your 'choices child' to simply 'do it' and you aren't giving them the choice not to. I quite like to use *hypnotic embedded commands* in situations like this.

'I'm wondering which book you'll read when you've brushed your teeth.'

Note that you're giving them choice on one thing but not on the teeth brushing. By using 'when' you're telling them that this is non-negotiable and you expect them to do it. Similarly:

> 'I'm wondering which video game you'll be playing with your
> friends when you've finished your homework.'

'I'm wondering' is the hypnotic part and should be said with the head tilted to one side in a curious sort of way so they focus on the 'wondering' bit while they hypnotically do the non-negotiable part of the instruction.

Other suggestions are to use the '*yes tag*'.

'I'm sure you want to do your homework as quickly as possible so you have a nice long time to play your video games with your friends, don't you?'

'You'll put your toys away now, won't you?'

It's all about giving choice, or appearing to, when they don't have one.

When I'm working with a child who struggles with this concept and wants choice or process and is being offered the opposite of what they want, I use something like the Story Cubes to invite my client to create a story where they have a choice even though they don't appear to have one, or a process when they are given choice. By creating scenarios with the Story Cubes, it gets them thinking more creatively as to how they can manage different situations they regularly face at school or home.

A really important metaprogramme that I tend to spend some time on is *towards and away from*. The reason it is important is because the brain wants to know what you DO want and it can get confused when we tell it what we don't want or what we want less of. Do you remember this from earlier on in the book?

Don't think about pink elephants!

What are you thinking about?

Of course – pink elephants.

The reason is that in order to understand the instruction, we have to be able to imagine a pink elephant, so our brain creates that thing. Now we are doing what we've just been told not to do. So when we say to our child:

'Don't talk in class.'
'Don't look out of the window.'
'You don't want to get a bad mark do you?'

...they are already thinking of this and creating that result in their head.

Therefore, it is scientifically known that thinking positively and focusing on what you do want, our 'towards' thoughts, will make us healthier and have more happiness and success in life than thinking about what we don't want.

Worrying about what we don't want, such as 'not having any friends in my new school', 'no one talking to me at the party', 'not getting the present I want at Christmas', 'getting a bad mark in the test', are all 'away from'.

Instead we need to *reframe* these as 'towards'.

'I am looking forward to making friends at my new school.'

'I'm going to talk to lots of my friends at the party.'

'I hope I get the present I want for Christmas.'

'I am going to get a good mark in the test.'

When you find yourself thinking about what you don't want or want less of, reframe it by thinking what you DO want. If your child starts saying, 'Mum I don't want...' Ask them what they DO want.

As a kids' coach I find child clients frequently start by telling me what they don't want.

o Teachers telling them off
o Mum or Dad shouting at them
o Their sibling taking their things
o Friends being mean to them
o Getting bad marks

Focusing so much on what they don't want makes them miserable and grumpy and more likely to actually attract that thing they don't want.

Just as this metaprogramme focuses on what we want more of/ towards and what we want less of/away from, the next one focuses on sameness and difference.

This is the *Match/Mismatch* pattern. We 'match' when we notice how things are similar, someone we are talking to perhaps, our opinions, mannerisms, language patterns and metaprogrammes. When we notice similarity, we find it easy to be in rapport because we easily understand what's being said and agree with it because the sentiments are similar to our own. Sometimes we might even finish each other's sentences. 'Mismatch' is the opposite, when we notice how we disagree with the other person, how we are different and our language pattern is so different we could almost be speaking another language.

Example

A nine-year-old girl told me that 'every day' (note the generalisation there) she sat on the bench in the playground because 'no one' (another generalisation) liked her or wanted to talk to her (note the distortion). She said she sat on the bench feeling very sad and lonely.

I asked her to show me what happened from the moment she walked into school. I thought she looked grumpy rather than sad.

I suggested that I would like to show her how she looked so I copied what she'd shown me.

I then asked, 'If you were in the playground and saw me walk in like that and sit there, what would you think?'

She said, 'I'd think you didn't want to play with anyone and that you wanted to be left alone.'

Now she could see that she was projecting the opposite of what she felt. She was focusing on what she didn't want and making that her reality. This is the Law of Attraction and children understand this very well. They totally 'get' that what you put 'out there' is what you attract, what you get more of.

So my client played out our little drama again, this time thinking about the positive result she wanted to happen. She looked like a different girl! She also said it felt much better. She hadn't enjoyed looking and feeling miserable and lonely, and she could completely understand how it hadn't worked, so another strategy was needed. We discussed 'if you always do what you've always done, you'll always get what you've always got' and she did wonder why she just kept repeating behaviour that didn't work.

The easy way to notice this pattern is when we think of 'match' as 'Yes, and...' and 'mismatch' as 'Yes, but...' The 'but' signals disagreement or mismatching. It breaks rapport and breaks state such that it draws attention to the mis-matcher who has broken the flow of the conversation. As such it can be a useful way to get attention when there's so much agreement that nothing is happening, no decision is being made because everyone is having such a lovely rapport-ful conversation!

Some children want to match, they want to get on with others and don't want to stand out or disagree. Sameness matters so they will find change difficult. Suddenly finding that they have a different teacher or have to be in a different classroom, sit next to someone different, will make them feel uneasy and anxious. Such children need to be assured of what is still the same and focus on what is unchanged rather than what is different.

Others want to challenge the status quo, look for where something is wrong, where they disagree, find what is different and be curious about it. They are the children in a class who will notice if the teacher misses out something or says something different from what is expected. They'll be the ones saying, 'But you said yesterday...' I have often found mis-matchers to have quite a scientific mind. On the whole, they embrace change as being a new opportunity and they get bored easily.

Many matching children are thought to be too compliant and easily get upset by confrontation at school and home. They seek harmony. Mismatching children thrive on discord and find it challenging so if you are the parent of such a child or the teacher, the best response is to simply find it curious, not take it personally and say 'It's interesting that you have that point of view, I don't have that point of view.'

Exercise

Whilst mismatching children could well become great scientists one day, in the meantime they have to fit in at school and they still want to have friends. So I introduce them to the word association game so they can experience how life is as a matcher.

You say a word and they have to say another word associated with it, and so on.

Example: Bread Roll Cheese Milk Tea Coffee Drink Biscuit Cake Birthday Presents and so on.

They are soon laughing as they enjoy some rapport that they don't usually experience.

I suggest they practice agreeing and see how that works for them in small ways at school.

I hasten to add that mismatching is not 'wrong' and that it is by noticing what's wrong that doctors, surgeons, and scientists heal people. It's how editors ensure the grammar and spelling is correct in books and how accountants check that you have entered an expense in the right category. Mismatching has great uses, so children need to learn how to be flexible and choose when they match or mismatch.

Another pattern that I find useful to teach children is the *Associated/ Disassociated* pattern because it enables us to step away from a situation and see it as it is, without the emotion. When we feel the emotion of the other person (as we tend to as parents), we find it difficult to be objective and discover what really happened or to see both sides of the situation. It's the difference between being 'in the story' or the drama or being outside of it, able to observe and clearly see what's going on.

As coaches and teachers, we stand a little way apart, caring for the child yet not emotionally involved. Coaches and teachers don't feel a child's emotions as if they were their own.

And that is how it should be but it doesn't always make it easy to know how to move forward when one is caught up in it to such an extent.

A way to slightly separate yourself is to ask what they actually saw, what was said and what happened first, then next, and so on, rather than to focus on their interpretation or potential distortion of what happened.

The next one is *Internally referenced/ externally referenced* and this is about who we refer to for our judgement. It is ideal to be able to move up and down the scale, able to check in with ourselves by asking, 'Am I doing the right thing here?' or, 'Should I say this?' as well as being aware of what others think, and taking their thoughts into consideration. A lot of children spend rather too long and give too much attention worrying what their friends think and not enough focus on what they think themselves. As a parent, if your child complains that someone has said this or that ask them, 'And what do you think?'

It is helpful to know how you stand on all these metaprogrammes, how your partner stands and how your children stand. The reason is that in my experience we can communicate so much better when we know because we can match their pattern to create rapport and enhance understanding and ultimately compliance.

8

CALMING THE BUSY MIND
MINDFULNESS EXPLAINED,
WITH EXERCISES

Mindfulness reduces stress and decreases anxiety, making it an excellent tool for us to share with our clients, our children, and for us to use ourselves.

It is paying attention
In a particular way
On purpose
In the present moment
And without judgement

It is about noticing our thoughts and feelings, our body and the sounds and images around us. This is very hard to do! If adults sometimes find it hard, you can appreciate how hard it is for children. So when our attention wanders off, distracted by things we need to do and worries about the past or the future, we need to bring it back to the breathing and to the present moment with kindness, patience, understanding and acceptance.

There are seven attitudinal foundations of mindfulness and I find it helpful to go through them with children, discussing which one resonates most with them and how, by taking on that attitude, they might change something that isn't going well for them. The seven attitudinal foundations are:

o Non-judging – be an impartial witness, a fly on the wall, a CCTV camera. It's about disassociation in NLP

o Patience – know that a resolution will emerge, the situation will develop and a solution will be clear

o Curiosity – use that amazing child-like imagination to be curious about what is happening

o Trust – that these are simply thoughts, they will pass

o Non- striving – allow the present to be what it is

o Acceptance – welcome what is

o Letting go – let go of control

I find this very helpful for parents, too. In fact, I've often started sessions with a mindfulness exercise such as the body scan below. It's perfect for those parents who fly in through the door, squeezing this time for themselves between errands, work and wanting to make the most of the session, almost talking to you about the problem before their bottom has reached the chair. This really isn't the best state, in my opinion, for them to work with me and it also creates a negative charge to the therapy room which the practitioner wants to avoid picking up themselves.

I usually use essential oils, something like Frankincense or Serenity in the diffuser for parent clients and encourage them to breathe, drink some water (great for any energy work such as EFT) and 'arrive'.

How often do parents feel the kids are pushing their buttons? Mindfulness helps them to notice these patterns and gives them the ability to respond calmly with greater clarity. When we learn to notice and rid ourselves of our habit of judging, fixing and doing, we gain freedom to be in the present moment where we need do nothing. Our mind does wander off into doing, that's normal and it takes daily practice to build up to a decent amount of time, say 15 minutes a day.

When your mind wanders off, just notice it. I tend to say, 'Here we go again!' and return my focus to my breathing. Like any muscle, it needs repeated practice to strengthen the neural pathway, changing your brain and making it easier each time.

I love this from Jon Kabat Zinn:

'Use your breath as an anchor to tether your attention to the present moment. Your thinking mind will drift here and there, depending on the currents and winds moving in the mind until at some point, the anchor line grow taut and brings you back.'

Here are some great ways to show children how to introduce mindfulness into their day.

a) Inhabit the pause

What this means is to consciously stop what they are doing, close their eyes and take a mindful break. I would recommend this to practitioners starting out who fear failure. Come on, we all do, don't we, at some time or another? Whether it be a new client, a case you've not encountered before, or just simply being tired, upset or not in a good place to be at your best.

Exercise
'Stop and put your attention to what you feel. I like to close my eyes and put my hands to my chest. We call this "tuning in".'
  I do this too so they can see what I mean.
'What do you feel?'
'Where in the body do you feel it?'
'What colour is it?'
'If there was a colour you could breathe in to lighten and brighten that colour, what would it be, just guess?'
'Imagine breathing in that colour through your head, down through your neck, your shoulders, your chest, your tummy, your legs and down through your feet into the ground, grounding you with this new colour. Now take that colour back through your legs, your tummy, your chest and into your heart. Fill your heart space with that colour and then when it's full, burst it out into your energy field so you are surrounded with that lovely colour. When you're ready open your eyes and come back to the room.'
  Explain that connecting mindfully with their feelings and breathing in a colour to lighten and brighten them, is a short exercise that they can do whenever they need to, anywhere.

Exercise
Body Scan

This is another exercise I will show children in a session. I ask them to put their feet on the floor, sit back in their chair and close their eyes.

'I want you to breathe in for the count of three 1-2-3 and out for the count of three. Focus on your breath as you imagine it fulling your heart space.

'Now imagine there is a beam of light energy coming from your eyes and shining on your big toe of your left foot. Take that light across your toes and under your foot, around your calf and shin and up to your knee.

'Now feel the heat from your left hand as it rests on your left thigh. Go to your left bottom and feel the pressure of it on the chair where you're sitting. Take that beam of energy up your back, gently flexing it to remove any stiffness and take it up to your left shoulder.

'Shrug your left shoulder a few times, roll it forwards and back then take the light energy up to your neck and rock your head side to side and forwards and back to ease any stiffness there.

'Now tighten all the muscles in your jaw, squidge your nose up and tightly close your eyes and open then a few times.

'You're ready to come down the right side so go down to your right shoulder and shrug it a few times, roll it forwards and back and come down your back again, flexing it like before. Feel your right bottom on the chair and feel its pressure.

'Take the beam of energy round your hip and along to where your right hand is resting on your right thigh. Feel its heat. Now follow that beam of energy down your shin and around your calf. Take it around your foot, along your toes and end up at the big toe of your right foot.

'Notice your breathing and the stillness of your mind and body as you open your eyes and come back to the room.'

Inhabiting the pause is about stopping and stilling the busy mind, the 'not wanting' or judging mind that says we 'should' or we 'must' that pushes us forward into our masculine energy to achieve and 'do'.

When we let go of this desire to get it right, to fix, we gain freedom. This is such a gift for your clients and only when you embrace the concept and incorporate it into your daily routine, can you authentically introduce it to your clients. Certainly, many of them have done a little mindfulness at school but I have yet to meet a child who does it outside school.

So many children have difficulty getting to sleep or staying asleep, they lie there worrying about their day or what tomorrow will bring. They are in the past and in the future. Instead show them how to be fully in the present.

This is something you can do anywhere, in bed if you can't get to sleep or if you wake up in the night and want to get back to sleep.

You can combine it with the previous exercise and suggest they breathe in a colour for calm, whatever colour calm is for them.

I love this quote from Jon Kabat Zinn, the founding father of mindfulness.

'The present is the only time that any of us have to be alive, to know anything – to learn – to act – to change – to heal.'

Children don't have much control over their life; it is dictated by parents and teachers. Showing them that they can control their breathing and their mind, is a powerful tool you're giving them because by doing this, they are 'at cause' rather than being 'at effect'. When we are 'at cause' we have choices to choose what is best for us whereas when we are at effect, we are living our life as victims with no choice.

b) Take it slow

I love this one!

I have a number of exercises, all involving slowing things down but by far the one that kids like best is 'eating the chocolate biscuit'. You could use a raisin or indeed a chunk of chocolate, much will depend on whether your client has any allergies and what their mum will allow. We are talking here about just a small piece, not a whole bar.

Exercise

Take your piece of chocolate and place it on the table in front of your client. I say:

'Do you ever find that your mind is just buzzing with so many thoughts? They could be thoughts about what you have to do still, things that went wrong in the day, worries about tomorrow, feelings you can't get out of your mind?

'I'm going to show you a way to slow this right down so you can feel calm. Today we're going to use a piece of food. We are going to very slowly discover how it looks, sounds, feels, tastes and let all the sensations of eating it last as long as we can. Our focus will be entirely on the piece of chocolate as if we are an alien who has never seen anything like it before. We are going to approach it with curiosity and enjoy every aspect of it.'

See it – look at it as if you've never seen anything like this before, notice its shape, its colour, size, texture, the edges, surface, pattern – what can you tell me about it?

Hear it – does it have any sound?

Smell it – without touching it, smell it, how does it smell?

Feel it – use the tip of your finger to feel all over it, the edges and the surface, how does it feel?

How did it get here? – imagine the process it took from the ground – production – the people involved – distribution – warehouse – shop – basket – home – table.

Taste it – lick the surface and just keep that taste on the tongue, where else can you get that taste sensation? Anywhere else in the mouth? Now move the tongue around your mouth, where can you taste it? Any sensations in the throat or the back of the mouth? Taste it again and take it further back in the mouth? Now taste it and move it to the side of your mouth. Is there any difference?

While you're doing this exercise with them, notice how their voice will get lower, movements slower and calmer.

Ask them how they feel, have their thoughts slowed down?

They can take this approach to many different activities as well as using it when eating. They can decide to eat one item of food a day, in a mindful way perhaps. They can shower mindfully, brush their teeth, walk in the garden, anything. It's about slowing it down and being hyper conscious of every part of the process using all their senses.

MAKING A MINDFULNESS JAR

A great way to introduce children to the concept of stilling the busy mind is to make a mindfulness jar.

Exercise

Take an empty jam jar and fill it with water.

Now have different colour pots of glitter and ask your child to think about their emotions and as they say an emotion, they choose which colour glitter to shake into the jar and how much of it to represent how much of that emotion they feel. They do this for other emotions until the jar has lots of different colour glitter in it.

Then talk about how sometimes they might get a really busy mind with so many emotions that they just feel overwhelmed.

As you talk about this with them, put the top on the jar and ask them to shake it as if they were feeling like this now. They will see all the glitter fill the water so it becomes murky and full of moving glitter as they shake the jar.

Now ask them to put it down and watch as the glitter settles and eventually the water goes clear. This is like mindfulness. We stay still just focusing on the present moment as our thoughts settle and clear.

9

ESCAPING THE DRAMA TRIANGLE

The Drama Triangle was developed by Dr Stephen Karpman in 1968 when he was a student of Eric Berne, creator of Transactional Analysis (TA). Like TA, The Drama Triangle is also a model using three positions, or roles. In this case: victim, rescuer, persecutor. It is a model that helps us to understand how conflict arises between people in intense situations (such as in families) but is equally relevant in all areas of life. Our focus here is obviously families.

You can use this in many ways:

o As a webinar, workshop, training module for colleagues
o In school as a workshop for PSHE or as a drama exercise
o Workshop for mum and dads
o Family workshop
o To help children and teens understand the role they appear to be colluding in

Most often, I use the Drama Triangle when it comes up naturally in a therapy session with a child. As a parent you may find yourself recognising the different roles within your family and the way family members move between roles, the role they play most often and you will also know the triggers. You can use the exercises with your own child in just the same way as one would with a client although for me, working with my own children has never been as successful as working with other people's!

As a coach I may have noticed 'victim' type language or the client may have described persecutor/rescuer behaviour patterns of parents or a bully in the playground. Sometimes I identify a 'drama triangle' pattern when observing the child with Mum or Dad, or suspect it from the initial email or phone enquiry.

So, what do you do if you identify with this pattern?

Firstly, I would point it out but in a general way, i.e. "Have you heard about the Drama Triangle?

No?

I then go on to explain that many fairy stories are based on this triangle or story structure whereby there is someone who wants something but can't get it (victim), the person or situation that they blame for this (persecutor) and how they are saved (rescuer).

Different cultures have their own folklore so you must choose a fairy story that your clients will know. I tend to use Cinderella.

I ask them if they know the story of Cinderella and ask them who they believe is the victim, who is the persecutor, and who is the rescuer. We usually get Cinderella as the victim or 'poor me' character who wants to go to the ball. The ugly stepsisters are the persecutors as they are preventing her from going, and of course the fairy godmother is the rescuer who waves her wand and we have a beautiful gown, a coach and off she goes.

Other fairy stories also have this construct, such as Snow White/ stepmother/dwarves or Red Riding Hood/Wolf/Woodcutter and so on. The idea is for them to understand the dynamic and start to get the ideas of which role they most often step into as their pattern.

I should point out that many of us therapists, coaches, or trainers may identify with the rescuer role so be aware that we all can fall prey to this Drama Triangle!

This is the classic triangle we recognise but, in reality, unless I am delivering a workshop and am prepared, I usually just end up drawing a triangle with a felt pen on paper in front of them. This has the additional benefit that we can write notes on it for them to take home and for me to photograph for my records.

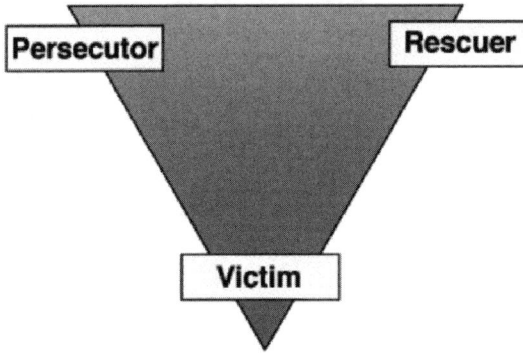

Having explained the concept using a fairy story I then move it into our session by explaining that a drama triangle occurs when there are three people taking the roles of victim, persecutor and rescuer. We call this a 1-down and 2-up role where two of the roles have power and one does not.

The 1-down is victim and the 2-up roles are persecutor and rescuer. I then ask them whether they recognise this in their own life, family or at school. Here's how this might go.

Coach – *Point at the Victim on the diagram in front of them.* Can you think of a time recently when you felt like a victim?

Client – Describes the situation.

Coach – How did that feel?

Client – Describes how they felt.

Coach – *Point to Persecutor on the diagram.* Who played the role of persecutor in that situation?

Client – Names persecutor or situation.

Coach – *Point to the rescuer.* Who or what was the rescuer?

Client – Names rescuer.

Now that they have understood the concept and related it to themselves, I want them to get a deeper understanding before we move into the process of how to step away from it. Here's how I explain it to them.

EXPLANATION

The *victim* is often described as the 'poor me' role. It is important to note that one can be in a victim type situation such as having a broken leg or having an illness, parents splitting up, but this doesn't mean that you <u>are</u> then a victim. Victim is <u>an attitude of mind</u> about your situation not the situation itself. I'm sure we can all think of people in dire circumstances who still remain optimistic and have a 'can do' attitude.

Here are some of the ways victim language is expressed:

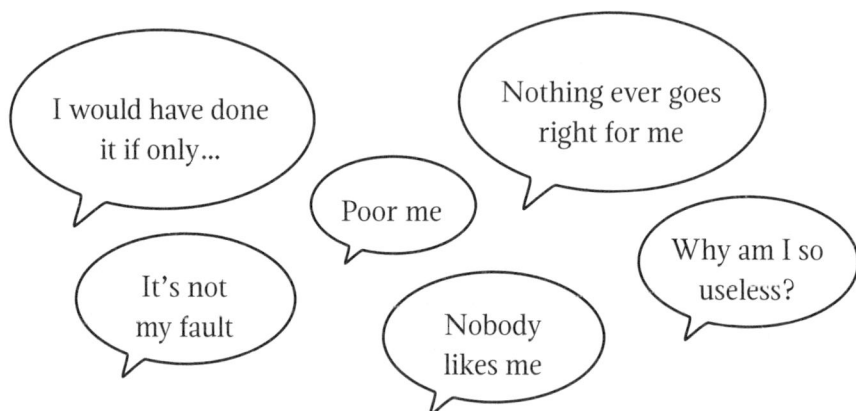

I would have done it if only...

Nothing ever goes right for me

Poor me

It's not my fault

Nobody likes me

Why am I so useless?

Has your child ever said things like that? The chances are that they have.

The *persecutor* is who or what they blame for them feeling like a victim in that moment. Persecutor is most likely to be a person but could also be a situation as I have just explained.

Interestingly, we usually find that the persecutor role has previously been in the victim role. They've got frustrated feeling like a victim and they need to fight back for their own self-preservation, and so they blame others or blame the situation.

How do we recognise the persecutor? As I've said, they often start out as victims feeling out of control and lacking self-esteem. No one is listening to them because they are not expressing their needs clearly and assertively. They don't believe that what they have to say is important and give responsibility to those around them rather than taking it on for themselves. They take out their frustration on others. These are people who separate themselves, even temporarily, from their emotions and distance themselves. They blame everyone else for the situation they are in and when you ask them what's the matter they say, 'Nothing.' In the persecutor role they are angry, either overtly or passively aggressive. Persecutors want to control and do this by nagging, putting others down and humiliating people.

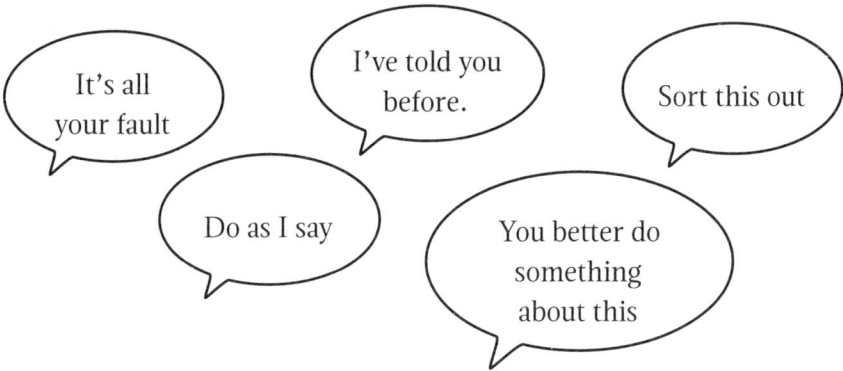

It's all
your fault

I've told you
before.

Sort this out

Do as I say

You better do
something
about this

Again, you ask your client, 'When have you been in this situation, blaming others, shouting and getting angry?'

I've had many clients turn to me and tell me they haven't in which case I ask, 'What, you've never been angry at your brother or sister, or shouted at your mum or dad?' and they sheepishly admit that they have. Ask them to remember that time and ask them what had happened just before they got really angry. They will undoubtedly remember having felt like a 'victim' just before.

The *rescuer* is the person or thing they turn to in order to be fixed, so it is most likely to be Mum, Dad or a teacher, but it could be food, alcohol or a friend. The rescuer focuses on other people's problems because it helps them to feel better about themselves. They feel needed and important. It raises their self-esteem at the expense of the victim. They think they know best. They are a fixer – 'What would he do without me?' They present as the 'goody', the 'nice guy' and hook into the victim who may feel overwhelmed. So, the rescuer feels needed and the victim has someone to take care of them.

Now when working with parents you will find that they defend the rescuer role by saying that it is totally natural. 'It's what parents do, isn't it?' My answer to this is that whilst we might do that out of necessity when our children are small, it can be inappropriate once your child is preparing to transition to secondary school, they need all the self-esteem they can get. If a parent is still rescuing them, this only benefits the parent, not the child.

The rescuer is not all that she (it is usually a female role) would appear. The rescuer actually gets her sense of self-worth from attempting to fix the problem and having her child dependent on her. Their positive intention is to feel important and necessary rather than having a genuine desire to help. They seek out people who are needier, more dependent than themselves, and they keep the victim in this dependent state by taking care of them. They consciously seek to find someone to rescue in order to feel important, and they believe they have all the answers. They volunteer for everything but then feel resentful and 'put upon' and frequently switch to the persecutor role if they are not getting the appreciation and positive attention they seek. The rescuer enjoys manipulating people into feeling guilty and dependent on them. They will say whatever needs to be said to keep everyone happy and avoid any negative attention on them.

The pattern you often see in families, and maybe you've experienced it yourself, is when you as parent and rescuer get fed up of taking all the responsibility, cleaning up for everyone, remembering their sports kit (having washed it), helped with homework, bought birthday presents for their friends and so on and not feeling appreciated. You then move to the persecutor role, often blowing up over some trivial thing. You then feel mortified and bad about yourself and move back to the victim role ('I'm such a bad mum/dad') possibly rescued now by a glass of wine, or a chat with a friend.

Shall I do that?

I just wanted to help

Anything to keep the peace

I like to feel needed

If I don't do it who will?

Do you want to talk about it?

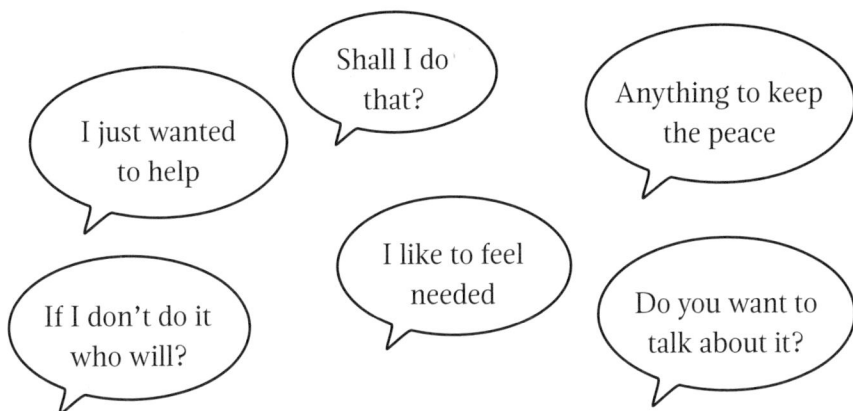

I imagine you recognise this dynamic and have yourself played all these roles at one time or another. The reason this dynamic plays out at home more than at work is because the family is the safest place to express our anger and frustration, and because, as a parent, particularly as a mother, we have a nurturing instinct especially when our children are young; it can be hard to let that go as they get older.

I set up and ran a Montessori School when my children were of preschool age and one of the key principles of Montessori is about children, even very young ones, taking age-appropriate responsibility. Here's what Maria Montessori says on this subject:

'An educational method which is based on liberty must intervene in order to help the child regain it; that is, to lessen as far as possible the social bonds which limit his activity... That is why the first form of educational intervention ought to have as its object the leading of the child along the path of independence. One cannot be free without being independent.'

— *Maria Montessori, 1972*

The problem with the Drama Triangle is that it is unhealthy from a mental and physical point of view because it is a continuing and repetitive pattern of behaviour in which no one actually gets their own needs met. It is draining of energy and leads to low self-esteem for everyone in it.

PATTERNS

In families one often sees a triangle where the child takes it upon themselves to be the victim. Mum rescues. Dad then decides he can't have this and turns into the persecutor to get the child to 'man up' and take some responsibility. The more he persecutes, the more Mum will rescue and the more helpless the child will feel especially as Dad may persecute Mum for rescuing, so Mum becomes Victim. Now the child tries to rescue Mum for which he'll probably be persecuted by Dad. These childhood patterns can unfortunately be continued into adulthood as victim children become victim teenagers seeking out a persecutor in the form of an abusive relationship.

Patterns tend to emerge in families and members tend to gravitate towards one role or another which can become their identity. Often, they begin in childhood with the eldest child becoming the *rescuer*. The word 'should' becomes their mantra but it can be hard work always being responsible for fixing and they can feel like a martyr and are at risk of burnout. They find it easy to know other people's needs but not their own. They worry about making the wrong decision or offending people. They suppress their anger until it blows up then they feel guilty and stuff it back down again, potentially causing digestive problems and migraine. They may have a distorted view of their responsibility and be over-responsible and taking on the responsibility for making their siblings happy.

The eldest child may switch to persecutor when frustrated in their role as rescuer, as they feel unappreciated and use blame and criticism in order to exert some control.

The youngest child often becomes the victim, overprotected by parents and older siblings. They have no opportunity to develop the self-confidence that comes from working out how to solve their own problems. They tend to be overwhelmed and anxious, and under-responsible.

But wherever we start, we end up feeling like a victim and feeling powerless. So we need a strategy to get out of it.

Exercise
Working with your client/child to step out of it.

1. Ask them, can you think of any times when you might have felt a bit like this victim? I often use characters like Moshi Monsters or LEGO figures here so that the child can pick a little character to represent themselves as the victim.
2. Who would be the Rescuer in their scenario? Pick another character to represent the rescuer.
3. And the Persecutor? Another character.
4. Ask them to tell the story, who did what?

5. *How did your client move around the triangle, what roles did they play?*
6. *How did it feel to be in each role?*
7. *What triggered them, what was said or done to make them move into the next role?*
8. *What could they have done or said instead?*
9. *What would have happened then?*
10. *Where would they prefer to be, inside or outside the Triangle? How do you think you could get outside it?*

Stepping out of the Triangle

Here are the steps that will help them break out of this triangle.

1. *They need to recognise that they are in one and want to break out of it.*

All the work you will have done with them will enable them to do this in future.

2. *Be aware of the triggers.*

What happens just before?
Is the trigger visual, auditory or kinaesthetic?
Do you consciously or unconsciously manipulate the situation? How?

3. *Decide now to break free of this Drama Triangle, step outside it.*

I usually suggest they take their Moshi Monster 'victim' character and hold it above the triangle I have drawn on the paper where we are working.
   This introduces them to the idea of disassociating, allowing them to emotionally distance themselves from what is going on.
   Suggested questions are:

o *Imagine you are looking down on this Triangle. What would you see?*

- o *What is happening, who is saying and doing what?*
- o *What would you suggest they each do?*
- o *What is your role in this triangle?*
- o *What good thing are you getting from it?*
- o *What is your good intention? Your compelling outcome? Your need?*
- o *How could you get the benefits another way?*

4. *How would it feel to take responsibility for having your needs met yourself?*

By now, you'll have set this session or workshop up so well that your client is totally willing to make changes, but you need to give them some more support because change isn't easy when a pattern is well entrenched.

Future Pacing

Go through some possible scenarios with them, things that could happen when they get home, later in the day, later in the week. Refer to situations they might have mentioned to you regarding their sibling, Mum or Dad.

- o What will they do differently?
- o How will they get better at recognising that trigger which sets off the Drama Triangle unfolding?
- o This could be an opportunity to set an anchor for the feeling they have when they take responsibility – proud, brave, happy, confident

No failure only feedback

Be prepared to make a few mistakes along the way – there is no failure, only feedback. They are making changes, so it may take some time to integrate the new behaviour for them and also for their family. It isn't easy when a child or teen has inhabited the 'victim' space in a family for so long. Will someone else jump in that space and play 'victim'? It will feel strange to take responsibility, and the rescuer will seek to take back control. It may be tempting to jump into 'persecutor' so remind them that this is all 'work in progress' with learnings along the way and that you will support them as they make these changes.

Victims need to become survivors

Encourage your client to think differently about themselves. You could use storytelling to ask about what a survivor might do if stranded on a desert island or something similar. I might use a sand tray for this, asking them to create their world using debris from the beach, whatever they can find and so on. Use shells, sticks, anything you have available.

o   Encourage resourceful thinking
o   What do they need?
o   What steps can they take to get it?
o   Chunk down the problems so they are manageable
o   Discuss afterwards what skills they've used to survive.
o   How could these skills help them in real life?
o   How much more confident do they feel now?

Rescuer needs to become a coach

It's difficult to stop parents wanting to help. Indeed, would we want to stop them really? No, we want to change things around so they do it with a different intent. Rather than controlling and fixing, the rescuer needs to gently hand back responsibility to the victim for fixing this themselves.

In the Montessori nursery, even very small children of 2 and 3 are able to push their chair back in, return a tray to the shelf, hang their coat up and so on. Teachers step back and let children do things for themselves and if something is dropped or spilt, then encouraging them to clear it up. In this way, children learn to be accountable for their actions and take responsibility. I remember my brother reminding my children (when they were very young) that there is no power without responsibility. This is so true, isn't it?

Good questions for the rescuer, going forward are:

'What would you like to see happen?'

'What do you think you could do to change this?'

Then they need to step back and let them make their own mistakes, being there for encouragement rather than providing the solution themselves.

Persecutor needs to acquire boundaries

When a persecutor learns to accept that it is not up to them to attribute blame, or to criticise, and that not everything is for them to control through anger and shouting, but by a softer, gentler, enabling approach, they will learn that trusting the process rather than controlling it will be a more effective approach.

Remind them that they have usually come from 'victim' and that by recognising the Drama Triangle earlier – and this applies to those who have arrived at 'persecutor' from 'rescuer' as well – there would be no persecutor role if victim and rescuer took responsibility for meeting their own needs.

Ongoing support

I encourage my clients to journal or keep a 'Gratitude Diary'. Other options which have worked well include: listing 3 things that have gone well that day before they go to bed, thinking in the morning of how well the day will go, and setting compelling outcomes such as 'I'm going to concentrate in maths today' or 'I'm going to go up and talk to Beth in the playground'.

A phrase I like to introduce to clients is this one:

'If you feed a man a fish you feed him for the day but if you teach a man to fish, you feed him for life.'

Exercise

Whether you identify with the victim role or know someone who behaves in this way, do this exercise to explore ways to exit the triangle.

Think of a situation where you have (perhaps without being aware of it at the time) put yourself in the victim role. Write about it here.

Who took the role of rescuer?

....

What did they do?

....

What did they say?

....

Who took the role of persecutor?

....

What did they do?

....

What did they say?

....

Did you move into the persecutor role?

....

In what way? How did you do that?

....

Now think about what you could do differently when that situation happens again. How could you take responsibility and exit the triangle?

> (empty box)

Exercise

All victims feel that they have been thwarted in some way, or that they have been prevented from achieving their dream. Of course, it was not their fault. Do you feel like this sometimes? Think about when you last felt like this and answer these questions about the occasion.

Q1. *Who were you blaming?*

....

Q2. *Why them?*

....

Q3. *What other choices did you have?*

....

Q4. *What other choices do you have now?*

....

Q5. *Are you ready to make these choices?*

....

(10)

TIME LINE TO HEAL PAST HURTS AND CHANGE THE FUTURE

Limiting beliefs and fears, anxiety and pretty much everything, stems from our time in the womb, our first six years and/or our ancestral, or possibly our past life. So it seems logical to use a Time Line to enable us to travel back in time to find it and heal that younger version of ourselves.

Exercise

Step 1. Ask your client to imagine a line along the floor and choose which end is past and which is future self. Then ask them to stand on a point that is where they feel they are right now. Ask them to share how they feel about the situation, fear, feeling etc. Now use the tapping process described in an earlier chapter. So ask where the feeling is, colour, SUDs level etc. Then start the set-up statement.

'Even though I feel... (colour and emotion) in my... I love and accept myself anyway.'

We do this three times, checking for any other feelings coming up.

Now lead them in two rounds of tapping using all the body and hand points using the reminder phrases.

Step 2. Ask, 'As you experience these feelings, can you take yourself back in time to when you had these feelings before?'

You're looking to the client to walk back into the past to the last time or a previous time when they had this feeling or belief, to their memory. We call their younger self with this memory – their inner child.

Step 3. When they stand at that point, ask them, 'How old are you now?' Then ask them to step off the Time Line and face their imagined younger self because we don't want them to BE them, we want them disassociated because we don't want them to experience the trauma again.

Step 3. So now they are looking at their (imagined) younger self. Here are some questions to check that they are disassociated and yet connected to that younger self. You don't need all these questions. The aim is to see their younger self and intuit what their younger self needs in this moment when something has just happened that has created the belief or decision that is the issue at the start.

- o *What is she/he wearing?*
- o *What is happening?*
- o *If they are frightened, you might need to 'freeze' a perpetrator.*
- o *You might need to get their mum.*
- o *What does he/she need right now?*
- o *Can you introduce yourself to her/him or do they recognise you?*
- o *Tell him/her that you're here to help them.*
- o *Do what needs to be done to make them safe.*
- o *Hug them (imagine there's a child there) to reduce the level of distress.*

Step 4. Ask, 'What is the belief or decision she/he made in this moment?'
The belief will sound child-like as we are speaking to the younger self so it could be something like
'Mummy doesn't love me.'
'I'm not important.'
'I get things wrong.'
'It's all my fault that Daddy left.'
'I'm stupid.'

Step 5. Now ask them what needs to happen to change this belief, maybe someone needs to do something different, explain something to someone. Invite them to make whatever changes need to be made to resolve the situation to change the belief/decision made. This can be done in silence. Tell them to let you know when this is complete.

You will probably notice a change in physiology and they will open their eyes and the client might say that they are OK now.

Step 6. Ask them to stand back on the Time Line where they just stepped off and check that their younger self is OK. They could rate it on a 0-10 scale where 10 is totally great.

If their score is less than that, ask them if their younger self wants to take them to a younger age when they had this feeling or belief.

Invite them to go to that place on their Time Line.

Step 7. Repeat the same process. What you're looking for is the earliest imprint of the negative belief because once you've changed this, you will be able to get your client to revisit each younger self and check that they are OK with each memory now.

Step 8. Now replay the memories to test that there are no negative beliefs around them any more. There may be other aspects of these memories though so you may need to do a Time Line again with your client, stopping at different aspects of the memory and other memories.

Once you get the best picture, imprint it like this.

'Can you see the positive picture? If this picture had a frame around it what colour would it be?

'What can you see, hear, feel, touch or taste in this new picture?

'What is the new feeling? The new emotion? And the new belief?

'Imagine bringing this new picture with its colour through your head, changing all the neural pathways and breaking old patterns, and then take this picture and the information through your body into every cell and fibre of your body, and then into your heart and send it out from your heart into your energy field and into the universe.

'When you're ready, come back to the room.'

Once you have done this with them, ask them to walk back along the Time Line to where they started, to their present self. Ask them to tune in to that situation, issue or feeling and check that it has now gone and been replaced by the new empowering belief or decision.

We then step into the future to a time when they have fully benefited from this new belief.

This is my favourite technique for overcoming limiting beliefs because children and teens haven't had their limiting beliefs for very long, even if for them a year feels like a lifetime.

o It's an active technique so they don't have to sit and talk, which they often prefer, and it tends to aid fast integration of the learning.

o It enables us to anchor the resourceful belief and 'future pace' by taking the new belief into the future or, in reality, the next school day.

o They can also recreate this at home whenever they want to and it's easy for you to do as a parent or teacher which makes it a great way to help children and teens find the best version of themselves.

If your client or child struggles to replace their limiting belief or negative emotions with positive ones, there could be a reason they are holding onto it. There may be resistance. Perhaps this has become their identity, maybe there is a positive payoff for keeping it?

I suggest saying:

'One of the NLP principles is that there is a positive intention behind every behaviour. If there was a positive intention, or some benefit of holding onto your limiting beliefs, what do you think it might be?'
Another expression for this is psychological reversal.

Good questions to ask are:
  – What does having this limiting belief enable you to do?
  – What does having this limiting belief get you out of doing?

At this point I might ask them to go to the time in the future when that limiting belief will have gone.

'Please go forward now along your Time Line to a point when you no longer have this Limiting Belief.'

I repeat the same process as we did with the past, after all, all our future selves are inside us as well.

I often find that because they are continuing to process all the time, by the time they go to their future self, the belief has already gone.

This process works so well because we are going back in time to when the limiting belief was imprinted and then clearing and changing it into a resourceful belief for our younger self. We then integrate it into our present and future self.

This process is taken from Matrix Reimprinting, a technique created by Karl Dawson and you can read more about it in 'Transform your beliefs. Transform your life' written by Karl Dawson and Kate Marillat. The entire process is much more complex but I use a trimmed down version here which works well with children and teens because they don't have quite so far to go back in time to when the belief was imprinted!

FINALLY

So now I've shared with you all my magical activities and exercises, tools and techniques that I've gathered over so many years working with wonderful children, teens and families.

I'd love to hear from you with your questions, suggestions, feedback because as I keep saying, that's how we learn and grow as people. We make mistakes, we pick ourselves up, dust ourselves off and keep going, improving all the time. You can get in touch via my website https://www.nlpfamily.com/. If you'd like to stay up to date with the activities I'm using and the ideas I have for working with children and teens, please subscribe to my newsletter full of information judybart.substack.com

OTHER GREAT RESOURCES

Five Love languages – 5lovelanguages.com
Gretchen Rubin Four Tendencies – Gretchenrubin.com
The Five Voices – 5voices.com
Olive Hickmott – empoweringlearning.co.uk
ANLP – anlp.org
Karl Dawson – efttrainingcourses.net
Kate Marillat – katemarillat.com
Philip Davis – Phoenixeft.co.uk
Sue Knight – sueknight.com
Judy Bartkowiak – For booking NLP or EFT Training, consultations for your family or just to have a chat nlpfamily.com

BIBLIOGRAPHY

Transform your beliefs Transform your life – Karl Dawson & Kate Marillat
Sue Knight – NLP at Work
Understanding Children's Drawings – Cathy A Malchiodi
The Art Therapy Sourcebook – Cathy A Malchiodi
The Secret World of drawings – Gregg M Firth
Do the Nattylala – Phil Reed & Annie Moodliar
The 5 side effects of kindness – Dr David Hamilton
The Science of Tapping – Dr Peta Stapleton
Magical New Beginnings – Sharon King

ACKNOWLEDGMENTS

I'd like to thank The London Writers' Salon, Parul Bavishi and Matt Trinetti for creating an amazing writers' community, bringing together writers of all genres, in every part of the world, several times a day with additional Midweek Mingle, Ship it Hour, Open Mic night and weekly Expert Hour with author interviews, masterclasses and pitch practice. How could I have written this without you?

Thank you to Karl Dawson for creating Matrix Reimprinting and training me in EFT, Kate Marillat for creating The Tapathon, running The Tapping Collective and her beautiful Soul Circles, Sharon King and Caroline Dawson for their training and Chrys Fisher for introducing me to EFT in the first place.

I must mention Sue Knight who was my NLP Trainer over many years, a constant inspiration, cause of much laughter and fun, insight and learnings.

Lastly a big thank you to Alice Solomons from Free Association Books who has been responsive, encouraging and enthusiastic on a daily basis. How do you do it?!

INDEX